THE NEW NINJA FOODI GRILL COOKBOOK

Easy-To-Make & Tasty Recipes For Indoor Grilling & Air Frying Perfection

BY

Chloe Coleman

ISBN: 978-1-952504-91-4

COPYRIGHT © 2020 by Chloe Coleman

All rights reserved. This book is copyright protected and it's for personal use only. Without the prior written permission of the publisher, no part of this publication should be reproduced, distributed, or transmitted in any form or by any means, including photocopying, recording, or other electronic or mechanical methods.

This publication is sold with the idea that the publisher is not required to render accounting, officially permitted, or otherwise, qualified services. If advice is required, it is necessary to seek the services of a legal or professional, a practiced individual in the profession. This document is geared towards providing substantial and reliable information in regards to the topics covered.

DISCLAIMER

The information written in this book is for educational and entertainment purposes only. Strenuous efforts have been made to provide accurate, up to date and reliable complete information. The information in this book is true and complete to the best of our knowledge. All recommendations are made without guarantee on the part of the author and publisher.

Neither the publisher nor the author takes any responsibility for any possible consequences of reading or enjoying the recipes in this book. The author and publisher disclaim any liability in connection with the use of information contained in this book. Under no circumstance will any legal responsibility or blame be apportioned against the author or publisher for any reparation, damages, or monetary loss due to the information herein, either directly or indirectly.

Table of Contents

INTRODUCTION 8

Meaning of Ninja Foodi Grill 9

Benefits of Using the Ninja Foodi Grill 10

Ninja Foodi Grill Accessories 12

Ninja Foodi Grill Functional Buttons 14

Steps to Use Your Ninja Foodi Grill 16

Useful Tips for Using your Ninja Foodi Grill 17

Ninja Foodi Grill Troubleshooting 18

Ninja Foodi Grill Frequently Asked Questions & Answers 19

Ninja Foodi Grill Breakfast Recipes 21

    Bacon and Egg Bite Cups 21

    Frittata 23

    Toad-in-the-Hole Tarts 24

    Sausage Casserole 25

    Sweet Potato Hash 26

    Bagels 27

    Apple Fritters 28

    French Toast Sticks 30

    Hash Brown Casserole 31

    Sausage Patties 32

Ninja Foodi Grill Poultry Recipes 33

Chicken Nuggets 33

Louisiana Style Shrimp 34

Grilled Shrimp 35

Bacon Wrapped Hot Dogs 36

Basil Lime Chicken 37

Perfect Steak 39

Cola Chicken 40

Bulgogi Chicken 41

Pulled Chicken Shawarma Sliders 43

Ninja Foodi Grill Beef & Pork Recipes 45

Roast Beef 45

Pork Chops 46

BBQ Pork for Sandwiches 47

Brown Sugar Meatloaf 48

Kalua Pork with Cabbage 49

Italian-Style Meatloaf 50

Meatball Nirvana 52

Pulled Pork Hatch Chile Stew 54

Ninja Foodi Grill Fish & Seafood Recipes 55

Garlic Shrimp with Lemon 55

Breaded Sea Scallops 56

Crumbed Fish 57

Alaska Salmon Bake with Pecan Crunch Coating 58

Baked Dijon Salmon 59

Barlow's Blackened Catfish 61

Perfect Fish 62

Ninja Foodi Grill Soup Recipes 63

Broccoli Soup 63

Cauliflower Cheddar 64

Cauliflower Couscous 65

Classic Pea Soup 66

Corn Soup with Chives 67

Minestrone Soup 68

Smoky Black Bean Soup 70

Thai Pumpkin Soup 71

White Bean Turkey Chili 72

Ninja Foodi Grill Rice & Pasta Recipes 74

Garlic Herb Rice and Chicken 74

Garlic Chicken Breasts with Pasta 75

Indian Rice Pilaf 76

Italian Sausage Pasta 77

Knorr Pasta Casserole 79

Knorr Pasta Side Chicken Flavored Fettuccine 80

Ninja Foodi Grill Beans & Grain Recipes 81

Green Bean Casserole 81

Ham, Green Beans and Potato Casserole 82

Bean Dip 83

Black-Eyed Pea Cheese Dip 84

Roasted Garbanzo Beans 85

Ninja Foodi Vegetable Recipes 86

Saffron, Courgette and Herb Couscous 86

Potato Soup 88

Easy Kimchi Fried Rice 90

Vegetarian Pulled Pork 92

Toasted Israeli Couscous with Vegetables 93

Ninja Foodi Grill Appetizer Recipes 95

Boiled Cajun Peanuts 95

Bourbon Infused Meatballs 96

Buffalo Chicken Dip 97

Buffalo Wings 98

Easy BBQ Meatball 99

Honey-Glazed Shoyu Chicken Wings 100

Honey Lemon Chicken Wings 101

Jalapeno Poppers 102

Meatballs with Spinach, Mushrooms Sauce 103

Mozzarella Stuffed Meatballs 104

Party Meatballs 106

Pillsbury Crescent Rolls with Pepperoni and String Cheese 107

Sausage and Cheese 108

Spinach Artichoke Dip 109

Steak and Beef Nachos 110

Ninja Foodi Grill Dessert Recipes 111

Baked Drunken Apples 111

Pumpkin Cake 113

Apple Cobbler 114

Banana Cupcakes 115

Black Bean Brownies 116

Blueberry Lemon Thyme Crisp 117

Cherry Dump Cake 118

Chocolate Cobbler 119

Chocolate Lava Cake 120

INTRODUCTION

The Ninja Foodi Grill is a kitchen appliance used in cooking delicious and sumptuous meals. It is one of the latest additions to a growing community of Foodi products. It does not only grill, it can also air fry, bake, roast, and dehydrate. The unit is big and boxy. The Ninja Foodi Grill is constructed of brushed stainless steel and has a black plastic domed lid. There's a grill grate, crisper basket, and a cooking pot which are coated with a ceramic nonstick finish.

The Ninja Foodi Grill as the name implies grill food with the lid closed. The lid doesn't press down on food but it only brands grill marks on one side at a time. The idea of the Ninja Foodi Grill air frying, bake, roast, and dehydrate makes it to overlap the normal Ninja Foodi Pressure Cooker and Ninja Foodi Oven.

However, the Ninja Foodi Grill is well constructed, the digital controls are easy to read and intuitive to navigate. It grills food excellently well without any smoke coming out from the unit.

Meaning of Ninja Foodi Grill

The Ninja Foodi Grill is a kitchen appliance used in cooking delicious and sumptuous meals. The unit circulates air around food for amazing Surround Searing and also the high-density grill grate creates food that's perfectly cooked on the inside and char-grilled on every side using Cyclonic Grilling Technology.

Ninja Foodi Grill is trying to outweigh the normal Air Fryer due to its multifunctional capacity which can bake, roast, air fry, or dehydrate. On most air fryers, you have to pull out a basket to toss and turn foods while frying; this can be awkward to hold the basket as you work. The Ninja Foodi Grill's lid opens upwards; it's very easy to access items that need to be flipped in the crisper basket.

Benefits of Using the Ninja Foodi Grill

1. **The Ninja Foodi Grill is very easy to clean.**

Cleaning the unit is not as difficult as you may think. The nonstick ceramic-coated grill grate, crisper basket, and cooking pot are all easy to clean and they are dishwasher safe in which you can deep the parts into water and wash it perfectly.

2. **Ninja Foodi Grill cooks faster.**

The unit uses high temperature of about 500°F to circulate rapid cyclonic air. This is what makes the Ninja Foodi Grill cook as fast as an outdoor grill.

3. **It grills delicious meals.**

Foods grilled with the Ninja Foodi Grill are crispier and more delicious than what you may have from the normal Air Fryer.

4. **The Ninja Foodi Grill cooks low fat meals.**

The grilling system of the Ninja Foodi Grill has a customizable protein and doneness settings which can enable you to perfectly cook food to your desired consistency and at a low-fat content.

5. **Ninja Foodi Grill has a dual sensor Foodi Smart Thermometer.**

This helps the unit to continuously monitor temperature during the cooking process. All cooking process is done at a given temperature.

6. **Ninja Foodi Grill is smoke free.**

The Ninja Foodi Grill was manufactured to work perfectly without any smoke coming out from the unit. This is one of its unique features. The combination of a temperature-controlled grill grate, splatter shield, and cool-air zone reduces smoke.

7. **Ninja Foodi grills food faster and healthy.**

With Ninja Foodi Grill, you can cook your favorite foods within some few minutes even without putting any oil.

8. **Ninja Foodi does not require you to flip the food over unlike Air Fryer.**

This mean you can confidently grill food like fish without waiting to turn over to the other side. Superheated airflow surrounds your food so you don't need to flip foods over like burgers. no sticking, no more falling apart. This is one of its unique features of the Ninja Foodi Grill.

9. **The digital control panel on the grill is easy to read and well designed.**

The Ninja Foodi Grill control panel is very easy to be understood. The unit needs to be preheated first before cooking for a better result. Preheating the unit can take up to 8 minutes.

10. **Ninja Foodi Grill parts are dishwasher safe.**

In the top of the lid, there's a splatter shield that needs to be cleaned after each use. Luckily, all of the removable parts (including the shield) can go in the dishwasher. The interior and exterior of the machine don't get particularly dirty, thus making cleaning easy with less stress.

Ninja Foodi Grill Accessories

1. **The Ninja Foodi Grill Unit.**

This part is responsible for cooking food at a very high temperature. To turn on, hit the power button on the front display and then select a cook function (grills, air crisp, dehydrate, roast or bake).

2. **The Hood.**

This always opens up to reveal the interior where different cooking accessories can be inserted. A splatter guard on the underside protects the heating element from grease. Cleaning it is very easy. Just make sure you have enough clearance to open the hood.

3. **Cooking Pot.**

The Ninja Foodi Grill pot is unique and dishwasher safe. The shape is like a deep roasting pan and it is inserted first into the Ninja Foodi Grill. It is used to hold drippings when grilling or air frying. However, the pot can also be used to roast or bake foods. Alternatively, you can even put a cake or pie pan inside to bake up a lovely dessert.

4. **Grill grate.**

This is another unique feature. It is dishwasher safe. It is inserted over the cooking pot for grilling and is part of the magic that helps the Ninja Foodi Grill superbly carry out those amazing grill marks. It has 2 handles on the side which allows for easy insert and removal. It is very easy to clean with some warm soapy dishwater and a scrub brush for sticky bits.

5. **Crisper Basket.**

The crisper basket is dishwasher Safe and is used whenever you want to air fry or dehydrate. However, the grill grate gets removed and the basket gets placed inside the cooking pot. It is very easy to remove and clean.

6. **Kebab Skewers.**

This makes cooking in the Ninja Foodi Grill fun. 5 skewers came packed inside the box for instant grilling fun. It is dishwasher safe and easy to clean.

7. **Cleaning Brush.**

This small cleaning brush is used to scrub and scrape crusted on bits left stuck to the grate and splatter shield after grilling. It is dishwasher safe and easy to clean.

Ninja Foodi Grill Functional Buttons

1. **Grilling.**

This is a unique and frequently used button. In order to test the grilling function, you can cook both fresh and frozen hamburgers, chicken breasts, salmon, and New York strip steaks and you will be very impressed at the result. The chicken and burgers will look like they were cooked on an outdoor grill.

Even without flipping over the fish to the other side, the skin on the salmon will be delightfully crisp and the top well browned. Steaks cooked in the Ninja Foodi Grill will come out better than many steaks broiled in an oven. One of the exiting aspects of grilling is that the Ninja Foodi Grill is entirely smokeless throughout the cooking cycle.

2. **Air Frying.**

Air frying food in the Air Fryer and Ninja Foodi Grill, the Ninja Foodi Grill rivals the best Air Fryers. Both fresh and frozen fries came out close to those fast-food ones that you find so irresistible. Cooking in most Air Fryers require you to pull out a basket to toss and turn foods halfway to cooking cycle and it can be awkward to hold the basket as you work. But as the Ninja Foodi Grill's lid opens upwards, it's very easy to access items that need to be flipped in the crisper basket.

3. **Roasting.**

If you dislike turning on your oven, you can roast a small portion of meat on the Ninja Foodi Grill. A pork loin roast can be roasted tender and juicy with a crackling crust.

4. **Baking.**

With the Ninja Foodi Grill, you can bake a cake because the cooking pot is large enough to hold an 8-inch pan. However, a yellow cake can be evenly browned with a moist tender crumb. The Ninja Foodi Grill could be a quick way to get a homemade dessert on your table.

5. **Dehydrating.**

The Dehydrating button is a very unique button which also helps to cook delicious food like apple rings. However, you can only fit about 18 slices onto the Foodi at a time which can yield about a cup and a half of dried apple rings.

If you like making your own dried fruits, even in small portions and you are also willing to leave the unit operating overnight, you'll be happy using the Dehydrating button and it will give you a nice result.

Steps to Use Your Ninja Foodi Grill

The Ninja Foodi Grill requires that you preheat the unit. Preheating the unit can take up to 8 minutes. For instance, if you wanted to cook boneless NY Strip steaks, ensure you use oil preferably peanut oil in order to enhance searing. The type of oil you use matters because it needs to have a high smoking point.

The next thing to do is to brush a light coating of generic vegetable oil and sprinkle on some Montreal Steak Seasoning. Set Grill Control on High temperature and allow the Ninja Foodi Grill to preheat for 8 minutes, you may add extra 8 minutes because the timer will start counting when the grill has preheated.

When the unit beeps to indicate that it has been preheated, an "Add Food" message is displayed on the control panel when the grill has preheated. You can now open the hood and place the steak on the Ninja Foodi Grill grate. Lock the hood and select Air Crisp. Grill for 8 minutes. The steak is ready to be served.

Useful Tips for Using your Ninja Foodi Grill

The Ninja Foodi Grill is very easy to be understood on how to use the appliance. The Air Crisp button works equivalent to a dedicated Air Fryer. In order to grill, you may add a small amount of oil, select Air Crisp mode and set the required temperature as long as the cooking time. You can begin the cooking process. Note, using the Air Crisp mode will not take you much time to properly cook the food but it will give you the optimum result you needed.

If the food you want to cook is more than what the Ninja Foodi Grill can contain in a single batch, you need to divide it and cook in two or three batches as the case may be. If you are cooking in batches, it's advisable you allow the unit to run for about 3 minutes between batches in order to reheat the grill grate.

The oil is important because it will aid in less smoke. It is recommended that you use oil with a high smoke point example canola, coconut, avocado, vegetables, or grape seed oil. Olive oil can cause the unit to bring out smoke. While you are cooking in batches, ensure not to overcrowd the food in the Ninja Foodi Grill grate or pot. Evenly arrange and space out ingredients in a single layer to ensure consistent browning and even charring.

You also need to monitor the food to ensure they don't get burnt due to the fact that the unit cooks food at a faster rate and at a high temperature. Note, the internal temperature keeps increasing as the food rest so you need to monitor the doneness with a food Thermometer.

When air fry crisping, check food and frequently shake crisper basket for a nice result. For a nice crispiness, use recommended oil for optimum results with fresh vegetable.

Ninja Foodi Grill Troubleshooting

1. **"E" pops up on the control panel display.**

When you see this, there's a problem somewhere. The unit is not functioning properly. Please contact Customer Service on 1-877-646-5288 the best assistance.

2. **"Add Pot" appears on the control panel display.**

This means that the pot is not properly installed in the unit.

3. **"Plug In" appears on the control panel display.**

This is caused by temperature probe. It needs to be plugged into the socket on the right side of the control panel. Before proceeding to cooking, ensure that it is plugged in the appropriate side.

4. **"Shut Lid" appears on the control panel display.**

This may happen even when the unit has completed its Grill preheating and it is time to add your ingredients. "Shut Lid" appears on the control panel display. If this happens, it means the hood is opened and needs to be closed for the selected function to start.

5. **Blinking lights appear after I press the START/STOP button.**

The blinking light is a progress bar indicating the preheating cycle.6. The preheating progress bar does not start from the beginning.

Note that from your previous use, when the unit is still warm, it will not require the full Preheat time.

6. **Can I cancel or override preheating?**

The answer is yes. You have to know that preheat is highly recommended for best results. However, you can skip preheating process by selecting the function again after you press the START/STOP button. If are using the grill function, you cannot override preheating process.

Ninja Foodi Grill Frequently Asked Questions & Answers

1. **Is the Ninja Foodi Grill easy to use and clean?**

The answer is yes. The control panel on the grill is well designed and easy to understand. The Ninja Foodi Grill preheats automatically and the preheat time can be over 8 minutes. In the top of the lid, it has a splatter shield that needs to be removed after each use and cleaned. All of the removable parts are dishwasher safe. The interior and exterior part of the unit is very easy to clean.

2. **Should I add my ingredients before or after preheating?**

The best thing to do is to preheat the unit right before adding the Ingredients.

3. **My unit is emitting smoke. Why?**

Please always use the recommended oil if you are using oil. Wrong oil can make the unit to smoke. If you are using the Grill function, ensure you select the recommended temperature setting. You can see the recommended settings in the Quick Start Guide and in the Inspiration guide. You also have to ensure the splatter shield is installed properly.

4. **How can I pause the unit to enable me check my food?**

The unit automatically pauses when the hood is opened during cooking process. If you want to pause the unit and check for proper doneness, what you need to do is to open the hood.

5. **If I put the cooking pot on my countertop, is it safe?**

If you do this, the pot will heat during cooking. Use caution when handling, and place on heat-safe surfaces only.

6. **Why did the unit burn my food?**

It is recommended that you put food into the unit when it has beeped to indicate it has been preheated. Always check the progress throughout cooking, and remove food when desired consistency has been achieved. To avoid burning, remove the food immediately the cooking cycle is completed.

7. My food didn't cook when I was using the air crisping mode.

Evenly arrange the ingredients in a layer on the bottom of the crisper basket with no overlapping. Ensure to shake loose ingredients while cooking for consistent crispiness.

8. Why is my food blowing around when I'm using air crisping mode?

You need to secure the loose food with toothpicks in order to avoid fan from blowing the lightweight foods around.

9. Can I Air Crisp fresh battered ingredients in the appliance?

The answer is yes. However, you need to use the proper breading technique. If you have flour, egg and bread crumbs to coat a particular ingredient, it is important to coat foods first with flour, egg, and then with bread crumbs respectively. Ensure to press the bread crumbs onto the food so they stick in place.

10. What can the Ninja Foodi Grill do?

As the name implies, the Ninja Foodi Grill can grill. It cooks food with the hood closed. Although the hood is closed while cooking, it doesn't press food down but it can only brand grill marks on one side at a time. The marks from the grill grate are curve not straight lines on the food. In the other hand, the Ninja Food Grill can also air fry, roast, bake, and dehydrate.

Ninja Foodi Grill Breakfast Recipes

Bacon and Egg Bite Cups

Preparation Time: 10 minutes

Cook Time: 15 minutes

Total Time: 25 minutes

Serve: 8

Calories: 332 kcal

Ingredients:

- ¼ Cup of shredded mozzarella cheese
- 3 Slices of cooked and crumbled bacon
- 6 Large eggs
- 2 Tbsp. of heavy whipping cream
- Salt to taste
- Pepper to taste
- ¼ Cup of chopped green peppers
- ¼ Cup of chopped red peppers
- ¼ Cup of chopped onions
- ¼ Cup of chopped fresh spinach
- ½ Cup of shredded cheddar cheese

Cooking Instructions:

1. Preheat the unit by Inserting the grill grate into the unit and lock the hood. Press Grill and set the temperature to Max.
2. Set the cooking time to 15 minutes. Press Start/Stop button. While the unit is preheating, beat the eggs into a small mixing bowl.

3. Add cream, salt and pepper. Give it a nice stir. Put half of the green peppers, red peppers, onions, spinach, cheeses, and bacon.
4. Pour the egg mixture into the silicone molds. Sprinkle the remaining half of all of the veggies.
5. When the unit beeps to indicate it has been preheated, place the mixture on the grill grate. Lock the hood and cook for 15 minutes.
6. Serve and enjoy!!!

Frittata

Preparation Time: 15 minutes

Cook Time: 20 minutes

Total Time: 35 minutes

Serve: 2

Calories: 412 kcal

Ingredients:

- 1 Onion
- 1 Pinch Spices, pepper, red or cayenne
- ¼ Lb. Turkey Breakfast Sausage
- 4 Egg
- ½ Cup of Mexican style cheese blend, Cheddar and Monterey Jack
- 2 Tbsp. Red bell Pepper

Cooking Instructions:

1. Preheat the unit by inserting the grill grate into the unit and lock the hood. Press Grill and set the temperature to Max. Set the cooking time to 20 minutes.
2. Press Start/Stop button. While the unit is preheating, combine together the sausage, eggs, Cheddar-Monterey Jack cheese, bell pepper. onion, and cayenne in a small mixing bowl. Mix thoroughly.
3. When the unit beeps to indicate it has been preheated, place the mixture on the grill grate. Lock the hood and cook for 20 minutes.
4. Serve and enjoy!!!

Toad-in-the-Hole Tarts

Preparation Time: 5 minutes

Cook Time: 25 minutes

Total Time: 30 minutes

Serve: 4

Calories: 388 kcal

Ingredients:

- 4 Egg
- 1 Tbsp. Chives, raw
- 1 Sheet of Puff pastry, frozen
- 4 Tbsp. Cheese, cheddar
- 4 Tbsp. cooked ham meat

Cooking Instructions:

1. Preheat the unit by inserting the grill grate into the unit and lock the hood. Press Grill and set the temperature to Max. Set the cooking time to 20 minutes.
2. Press Start/Stop button. While the unit is preheating, unfold the pastry sheet on a flat surface and divide into 4 squares.
3. When the unit beeps to indicate it has been preheated, place the pastry squares on the grill grate. Lock the hood and cook for 15 minutes.
4. Remove the grill grate and use a metal tablespoon to gently press each square to form a hole.
5. Place 1 Tbsp. of Cheddar cheese and 1 Tbsp. ham in each hole and pour 1 egg on top of each.
6. Return the grill grate to the unit and cook for more 10 minutes. Top tarts with chives. Serve and enjoy!!!

Sausage Casserole

Preparation Time: 10 minutes

Cook Time: 20 minutes

Total Time: 30 minutes

Serve: 6

Calories: 180 kcal

Ingredients:

- ¼ Cup Sweet Onion, diced
- 4 Eggs
- 1 Lb. Hash Browns
- 1 Lb. Ground Breakfast Sausage
- 1 Green Bell Pepper, diced
- 1 Red Bell Pepper, diced
- 1 Yellow Bell Pepper, diced

Cooking Instructions:

1. Preheat the unit by inserting the grill grate into the unit and lock the hood. Press Grill and set the temperature to Max. Set the cooking time to 20 minutes.
2. Press Start/Stop button. When the unit beeps to indicate that it has been preheated, place the hash browns on the grill grate.
3. Top with sausage, pepper and onions. Place the mixture on the grill grate. Lock the hood and cook for 20 minutes.
4. Beat the egg into a small mixing bowl and pour on top of the Casserole. Cook for another 10 minutes. Top with salt and pepper.
5. Serve and enjoy!!!

Sweet Potato Hash

Preparation Time: 10 minutes

Cook Time: 15 minutes

Total Time: 25 minutes

Serve: 6

Calories: 227 kcal

Ingredients:

- 2 Large Sweet potato
- 2 Slices of Pork
- 2 Tbsp. Olive Oil
- 1 Tbsp. Spices, paprika
- 1 Tsp. Sea Salt
- 1 Tsp. Spices (pepper black)
- 1 Tsp. Spices, dill weed, dried

Cooking Instructions:

1. Preheat the unit by inserting the grill grate into the unit and lock the hood. Press Grill and set the temperature to Max. Set the cooking time to 15 minutes.
2. Press Start/Stop button. While the unit is preheating, mix together the sweet potato, bacon, olive oil, paprika, salt, pepper, and dill in a large mixing bowl.
3. Place the mixture on the grill grate and lock the hood. Cook for about 15 minutes. Check for proper doneness.
4. Serve and enjoy!!!

Bagels

Preparation Time: 5 minutes

Cook Time: 4 minutes

Total Time: 9 minutes

Serve: 2

Calories: 245 kcal

Ingredients:

- 2 Bagels, opened for roasting

Cooking Instructions:

1. Preheat the unit by inserting the grill grate into the unit and lock the hood. Press Grill and set the temperature to Max. Set the cooking time to 4 minutes.
2. Press Start/Stop button. While the unit is preheating, open up the bagel if you want the bagel toasted inside. Close the bagel and lay it on the Ninja Foodi Grill grate.
3. Lock the hood and cook for about 4 minutes. Top with cream cheese or jam. Check for proper doneness.
4. Serve and enjoy!!!

Apple Fritters

Preparation Time: 15 minutes

Cook Time: 10 minutes

Total Time: 25 minutes

Serve: 4

Calories: 136 kcal

Ingredients:

- 1 Cup of all-purpose flour
- ¼ Cup of Sugars, granulated
- ¼ Cup of Milk
- 1 Egg
- 1 ½ Tsp. Leavening agents (baking powder)
- 1 Pinch of Salt, table
- 2 Tbsp. Sugars, granulated
- ½ Tsp. Spices, (cinnamon and ground pepper)
- 1 Apples, raw
- ½ Cup of Sugars, powdered
- 1 Tbsp. Milk, reduced fat
- ½ Tsp. Vanilla extract
- ¼ Tsp. Spices, cinnamon, ground

Cooking Instructions:

1. Preheat the unit by inserting the grill grate into the unit and lock the hood. Press Grill and set the temperature to Max. Set the cooking time to 10 minutes.
2. Press Start/Stop button. While the unit is preheating, combine together the flour, ¼ cup sugar, milk, egg, baking powder, and salt in a small bowl.

3. Combine 2 Tbsp. sugar with cinnamon in another bowl and sprinkle over apples. Pour the apples into the flour mixture.
4. When the unit beeps to indicate that it has been preheated, place fritters on the Ninja Foodi Grill grate and lock the hood. Cook for 10 minutes.
5. In a small mixing bowl, combine together the confectioners' sugar, milk, caramel extract, and cinnamon. Transfer fritters to a cooling rack and drizzle with glaze.
6. Serve and enjoy!!!

French Toast Sticks

Preparation Time: 10 minutes

Cook Time: 10 minutes

Total Time: 20 minutes

Serve: 2

Calories: 392 kcal

Ingredients:

- 4 Slices of Bread
- 2 Egg
- ¼ Cup of Milk
- 1 Tsp. Vanilla extract
- 1 Tsp. Spices (cinnamon and ground pepper)
- 1 Pinch of Spices

Cooking Instructions:

1. Preheat the unit by inserting the grill grate into the unit and lock the hood. Press Grill and set the temperature to Max. Set the cooking time to 10 minutes.
2. Press Start/Stop button. While the unit is preheating, cut each sliced bread into 3 and make sticks.
3. In a small mixing bowl, merge together eggs, milk, vanilla extract, cinnamon, and nutmeg. Dip each piece of bread into egg mixture.
4. Shake each bread stick to get rid of excess liquid and arrange them in the Ninja Foodi Grill grate. Cook for about 10 minutes.
5. Serve and enjoy!!!

Hash Brown Casserole

Preparation Time: 5 minutes

Cook Time: 30 minutes

Total Time: 35 minutes

Serve: 12

Calories: 187 kcal

Ingredients:

- 1 Lb. Ham
- ½ cup cheddar cheese
- 6 Eggs
- 48 Oz. bag frozen hash browns
- ¼ Cup of milk
- 1 Large onion
- 3 Tbsp. olive oil

Cooking Instructions:

1. Preheat the unit by inserting the grill grate into the unit and lock the hood. Press Grill and set the temperature to Max. Set the cooking time to 30 minutes.
2. Press Start/Stop button. When the unit beeps to indicate that it has been preheated, place onion, oil and frozen hash browns.
3. Sauté to your desired consistency. In a small mixing bowl, merge together the egg and milk and then pour the mixture on top of the hash browns.
4. Place the meat on the top. Put the hash brown on the Ninja Foodi Grill grate and lock the hood. Cook for about 30 minutes. Top with cheddar cheese.
5. Serve and enjoy!!!

Sausage Patties

Preparation Time: 5 minutes

Cook Time: 10 minutes

Total Time: 15 minutes

Serve: 4

Calories: 248 kcal

Ingredients:

- 1 (12 Oz.) Package of pork sausage
- 1 Serving Pam Butter Cooking spray

Cooking Instructions:

1. Preheat the unit by inserting the grill grate into the unit and lock the hood. Press Grill and set the temperature to Max. Set the cooking time to 10 minutes.
2. Press Start/Stop button. When the unit beeps to indicate that it has been preheated, place the sausage patties on the Ninja Foodi Grill grate.
3. Lock the hood and cook for about 10 minutes. Check for doneness by inserting Instant thermometer and it reads 160°F.
4. Serve and enjoy!!!

Ninja Foodi Grill Poultry Recipes

Chicken Nuggets

Preparation Time: 10 minutes

Cook Time: 10 minutes

Total Time: 20 minutes

Serve: 4

Calories: 188 kcal

Ingredients:

- 2 Tbsp. panko
- 2 Tbsp. grated parmesan cheese
- 16 Oz. 2 large skinless boneless chicken breasts, cut into even 1-inch bite sized pieces
- ½ Tsp. kosher salt
- Black pepper to taste
- 2 Tsp. olive oil
- 6 Tbsp. whole wheat Italian seasoned breadcrumbs

Cooking Instructions:

1. Preheat the unit by inserting the grill grate into the unit and lock the hood. Press Grill and set the temperature to Max. Set the cooking time to 10 minutes.
2. Press Start/Stop button. While the unit is preheating, combine together the breadcrumbs, panko and parmesan cheese. Mix thoroughly and add the oil.
3. Add salt and pepper. Give it a nice mix. Deep chunks of chicken into the breadcrumb mixture and coat well.
4. Place the chicken on the Ninja Foodi Grill grate and lock the hood. Cook for about 10 minutes. Serve and enjoy!!!

Louisiana Style Shrimp

Preparation Time: 5 minutes

Cook Time: 30 minutes

Total Time: 35 minutes

Serve: 4

Calories: 329 kcal

Ingredients:

- 1 Lb. medium shrimp-deveined
- ½ Cup of butter sliced
- 1 Lemon zest, juiced
- 1 Tbsp. Worcestershire sauce
- 1 Tsp. Old Bay Seasoning
- 1 Tsp. minced garlic
- ½ Tsp. salt
- ½ Tsp. pepper
- Savory Parmesan Rice

Cooking Instructions:

1. Preheat the unit by inserting the grill grate into the unit and lock the hood. Press Grill and set the temperature to Max. Set the cooking time to 30 minutes.
2. Press Start/Stop button. While the unit is preheating, zest your lemon with a zester into a small mixing bowls and then keep aside.
3. When the unit beeps to indicate that it is preheated, put the shrimp, lemon juice, Worcestershire sauce, seasoning, salt, pepper, garlic and butter to grill grate.
4. Lock the hood and cook the shrimp for about 30 minutes. When the cooking cycle is up, add 1 ½ Tsp. of lemon zest.
5. Serve and enjoy!!!

Grilled Shrimp

Preparation Time: 5 minutes

Cook Time: 5 minutes

Total Time: 10 minutes

Serve: 7

Calories: 146 kcal

Ingredients:

- 2 Lbs. Shrimp raw, shell on, deveined
- 2 Tbsp. olive oil
- 1 Tbsp. Lawry's Seasoned Salt
- 1 Tbsp. Old Bay Seasoning

Cooking Instructions:

1. Preheat the unit by inserting the grill grate into the unit and lock the hood. Press Grill and set the temperature to Max. Set the cooking time to 30 minutes.
2. Press Start/Stop button. While the unit is preheating, merge together all the ingredients in a small mixing bowl.
3. When the unit beeps to indicate that it is preheated, place the mixture on the Ninja Foodi Grill grate and cook for 5 minutes.
4. Serve and enjoy!!!

Bacon Wrapped Hot Dogs

Preparation Time: 10 minutes

Cook Time: 15 minutes

Total Time: 25 minutes

Serve: 8

Calories: 203 kcal

Ingredients:

- 8 Hot Dogs
- 8 Strips of Bacon

Cooking Instructions:

1. Preheat the unit by inserting the grill grate into the unit and lock the hood. Press Grill and set the temperature to Max. Set the cooking time to 15 minutes.
2. Press Start/Stop button. While the unit is preheating, begin to wrap each hot dog with desired amount of bacon.
3. When the unit beeps to indicate that it is preheated, place the hot dogs on the Ninja Foodi Grill grate. Lock the hood and cook for about 15 minutes.
4. Serve and enjoy!!!

Basil Lime Chicken

Preparation Time: 1 hour

Cook Time: 14 minutes

Total Time: 1 hour 14 minutes

Serve: 6

Calories: 445 kcal

Ingredients:

For marinade:

- 3 Lbs. Boneless Skinless Chicken
- Salt to taste
- Pepper to taste
- 2 Limes juice and zest
- 3 Tbsp. Dijon Mustard
- 3 Tbsp. Worcestershire Sauce
- 3 Tbsp. Soy Sauce
- 3 Tbsp. Olive Oil
- 3 Green onions, chopped
- 2 Cloves Garlic, minced

For dressing:

- 1 Lime juice and zest
- ¼ Cup Extra Virgin Olive Oil
- 3 Green Onions, chopped
- 2 Tbsp. Basil, chopped
- 2 Cloves Garlic, minced

Cooking Instructions:

1. Preheat the unit by inserting the grill grate into the unit and lock the hood. Press Grill and set the temperature to Max. Set the cooking time to 14 minutes.
2. Press Start/Stop button. While the unit is preheating, begin to merge together all the marinade Ingredients alongside with chicken in a small mixing bowl.
3. Allow it to marinade for an hour. When the unit beeps to indicate that it is preheated, place the chicken on the Ninja Foodi Grill grate.
4. Lock the hood and cook for about 14 minutes. When it is done, allow it to cool before cutting. Mix together the dressing Ingredients and coat the chicken with it.
5. Serve and enjoy!!!

Perfect Steak

Preparation Time: 30 minutes

Cook Time: 7 minutes

Total Time: 37 minutes

Serve: 2

Calories: 590 kcal

Ingredients:

- 20 Oz. Rib eye steak
- Steak seasoning to taste

Cooking Instructions:

1. Preheat the unit by inserting the grill grate into the unit and lock the hood. Press Grill and set the temperature to Max. Set the cooking time to 7 minutes.
2. Press Start/Stop button. While the unit is preheating, apply seasoning on the stick and keep it for sometimes.
3. When the Ninja Foodi Grill beeps to indicate that it is preheated, place the stick on the Ninja Foodi Grill grate and cook for about 7 minutes.
4. When it is done, remove the stick and allow it to cool before cutting.
5. Serve and enjoy!!!

Cola Chicken

Preparation Time: 8 minutes

Cook Time: 15 minutes

Total Time: 23 minutes

Serve: 4

Calories: 228 kcal

Ingredients:

- ½ Tsp. kosher salt
- Ground black pepper, to taste
- 1 Cup of ketchup
- 1 Cup of cola
- 1 Large onion, thinly sliced
- 4 Lbs. of chicken parts

Cooking Instructions:

1. Preheat the unit by inserting the grill grate into the unit and lock the hood. Press Grill and set the temperature to Max. Set the cooking time to 15 minutes.
2. Press Start/Stop button. When the unit beeps to indicate that it has been preheated, place half of the sliced onions on the Ninja Foodi Grill grate.
3. Add chicken, salt, pepper and the remaining onions. Merge together the ketchup and cola in a small mixing bowl. Stir thoroughly.
4. Pour the ketchup mixture on the chicken. Lock the hood and cook for about 15 minutes. When the cooking cycle is up, remove the chicken and shred with 2 forks.
5. Serve and enjoy!!!

Bulgogi Chicken

Preparation Time: 5 minutes

Cook Time: 15 minutes

Total Time: 20 minutes

Serve: 4

Calories: 306 kcal

Ingredients:

- 2 Lbs. boneless skinless chicken thighs, sliced into strips
- ½ Red onion, finely chopped
- 2 Cloves garlic, finely chopped
- 1 (15-gram) Piece of fresh ginger, grated
- ¼ Cup of scallion, finely chopped
- 3 Tbsp. soy sauce
- 1 Tbsp. gochujang
- 1 Tbsp. honey
- 1 Tbsp. toasted sesame oil
- ¼ Cup of mirina
- ¼ Cup of sesame seeds
- Green onions

Cooking Instructions:

1. Preheat the unit by inserting the grill grate into the unit and lock the hood. Press Grill and set the temperature to Max. Set the cooking time to 15 minutes.
2. Press Start/Stop button. While the unit is preheating, merge together all the ingredients in a small mixing bowl and stir thoroughly.
3. Put the chicken into the mixture to coat properly. Close the bowl and place in the Ninja Foodi Grill grate. Lock the hood and cook for 15 minutes.

4. When the cooking cycle is over, remove the chicken to a platter and top with green onions.
5. Serve and enjoy!

Pulled Chicken Shawarma Sliders

Preparation Time: 15 minutes

Cook Time: 20 minutes

Total Time: 35 minutes

Serve: 4

Calories: 225 kcal

Ingredients:

- 2 Chicken breasts
- 1 Tbsp. olive oil

For the Sauce:

- 1 Tbsp. olive oil
- 1 Small onion, diced
- 1 Cup of tomato sauce
- ½ Tsp. cumin
- ½ Tsp. coriander
- ½ Tsp. garlic powder
- ¼ Tsp. cinnamon
- ¼ Tsp. turmeric
- Pinch of cayenne pepper
- Salt
- Freshly ground black pepper (to taste)

Cooking Instructions:

1. Preheat the unit by inserting the grill grate into the unit and lock the hood. Press Grill and set the temperature to Max. Set the cooking time to 20 minutes.

2. Press Start/Stop button. When the unit beeps to indicate that it has been preheated, rub the chicken breasts with the olive oil.
3. Place the chicken on the Ninja Foodi Grill grate and cook for 6 minutes. Remove the chicken and set aside.
4. Add the olive oil, diced onion, tomato sauce, ground cumin, ground coriander, garlic powder, cinnamon, turmeric, cayenne, salt, and black pepper into the grill.
5. Shred the cooked chicken with two forks and add it to the grill. Lock the hood and cook for 9 minutes. Top with sliced red onions.
6. Serve and enjoy!!!

Ninja Foodi Grill Beef & Pork Recipes

Roast Beef

Preparation Time: 5 minutes

Cook Time: 35 minutes

Total Time: 40 minutes

Serve: 7

Calories: 238 kcal

Ingredients:

- 2 Lb. beef roast top round
- oil

Rub:

- 1 Tbsp. kosher salt
- 1 Tsp. black pepper
- 2 Tsp. garlic powder
- 1 Tsp. summer savory

Cooking Instructions:

1. Preheat the unit by inserting the grill grate into the unit and lock the hood. Press Grill and set the temperature to Max. Set the cooking time to 20 minutes.
2. Press Start/Stop button. While the unit is preheating, combine all rub ingredients and coat the beef with the mixture.
3. When the unit beeps to indicate that it has been preheated, place fat side down in the Ninja Foodi Grill grate. Lock the hood and cook for 35 minutes.
4. When the cooking cycle is up, remove the roast from the Ninja Foodi Grill and allow it to cool for 10 minutes. Serve and enjoy!!!

Pork Chops

Preparation Time: 5 minutes

Cook Time: 12 minutes

Total Time: 17 minutes

Serve: 4

Calories: 391 kcal

Ingredients:

- 8 Oz. pork chops
- 1 Tsp. olive oil

Seasoning:

- 1 Tsp. paprika
- 1 Tsp. onion powder
- 1 Tsp. salt
- 1 Tsp. pepper

Cooking Instructions:

1. Preheat the unit by inserting the grill grate into the unit and lock the hood. Press Grill and set the temperature to Max. Set the cooking time to 12 minutes.
2. Hit Start/Stop button. While the unit is preheating, brush bothsides of pork chop with olive oil.
3. In s small mixing bowl, mix together the pork seasonings and apply it on both sides of the pork chop.
4. When the unit beeps to indicate that it has been preheated, arrange the pork chop on the Ninja Foodi Grill grate.
5. Lock the hood and cook for about 12 minutes. Flip the pork chops onto a serving plate. Serve and enjoy!!!

BBQ Pork for Sandwiches

Preparation Time: 15 minutes

Cook Time: 4 hours 30 minutes

Total Time: 4 hours 45 minutes

Serve: 12

Calories: 465 kcal

Ingredients:

- 1 (14 Oz.) beef broth
- 3 Lbs. Pork chop
- 1 (18 Oz.) barbeque sauce

Cooking Instructions:

1. Preheat the unit by inserting the grill grate into the unit and lock the hood. Press Grill and set the temperature to Max. Set the cooking time to 4 hours 30 minutes.
2. Hit Start/Stop button. When the unit beeps to indicate that it has been preheated, pour can of beef broth and boneless pork ribs into the Ninja Foodi Grill grate.
3. Lock the hood and cook for 4 hours. When the cooking cycle is up, open the unit and stir in barbeque. Cook for another 30 minutes.
4. Serve and enjoy!!!

Brown Sugar Meatloaf

Preparation Time: 20 minutes

Cook Time: 1 hour

Total Time: 1 hour 20 minutes

Serve: 8

Calories: 374 kcal

Ingredients:

- ½ Cup of Sugars, brown
- ½ Cup of Ketchup
- 1 ½ Lb. Beef
- ¾ Cup of Milk, reduced fat
- 2 Egg
- 1 ½ Tsp. Salt, table
- ¼ Tsp. Black pepper Spices
- 1 Small Onions, raw
- ¼ Tsp. Ginger Spices
- ¾ Cup of Crackers, saltines

Cooking Instructions:

1. Preheat the unit by inserting the grill grate into the unit and lock the hood. Press Grill and set the temperature to Max. Set the cooking time to 1 hour.
2. Hit Start/Stop button. When the unit beeps to indicate that it has been preheated, Press the brown sugar in the Ninja Foodi Grill grate and spread the ketchup.
3. Merge together all the remaining ingredients in a small mixing bowl. Mix well and shape into loaf. Place on top of the ketchup.
4. Lock the hood and cook for 1 hour. When the cooking cycle is over, remove the Meatloaf and allow it to cool. Serve and enjoy!!!

Kalua Pork with Cabbage

Preparation Time: 10 minutes

Cook Time: 40 minutes

Total Time: 50 minutes

Serve: 10

Calories: 219 kcal

Ingredients:

- 1 Tsp. liquid smoke
- ½ Large head Cabbage
- 2 Tbsp. Morton Kosher Salt
- 2 Tsp. Spices, pepper, black
- ½ Tsp. Spices, ginger, ground
- 1 (5 Lbs.) Pork
- 1 Tbsp. Soy sauce
- 2 Tsp. Worcestershire Sauce

Cooking Instructions:

1. Preheat the unit by inserting the grill grate into the unit and lock the hood. Press Grill and set the temperature to Max. Set the cooking time to 20 minutes.
2. Hit Start/Stop button. While the unit is preheating, merge together kosher salt, black pepper, and ground ginger in a small mixing bowl.
3. Rub the mixture on the pork roast. When the unit beeps to indicate that it has been preheated, place seasoned roast on the Ninja Foodi Grill grate.
4. Lock the hood and cook for 20 minutes. Stir soy sauce, Worcestershire sauce, and liquid smoke together in a small mixing bowl.
5. Pour over the pork roast and add garbage. Cook for another 20 minutes. When the cooking cycle is over, remove the chicken and shred with two forks. Serve.

Italian-Style Meatloaf

Preparation Time: 15 minutes

Cook Time: 1 hour

Total Time: 1 hour 15 minutes

Serve: 4

Calories: 395 kcal

Ingredients:

- 1 ½ Lb. lean ground beef
- 1 Cup of soft breadcrumbs
- 2 Large garlic cloves finely minced
- ¼ Cup of onion finely chopped
- 3 Eggs
- 1 Tbsp. fresh oregano, chopped
- ¼ Cup of fresh parsley, chopped
- ¼ Cup of grated Parmesan
- 1 Cup of shredded mozzarella
- 3 Tbsp. tomato paste
- 2 Tsp. salt
- 1 Tsp. pepper

Sauce:

- 2 Cup of tomato puree
- ¼ Cup of chopped fresh basil
- 2 Tbsp. brown sugar
- ½ Tsp. salt
- ¼ Tsp. pepper

Cooking Instructions:

1. Preheat the unit by inserting the grill grate into the unit and lock the hood. Press Grill and set the temperature to Max. Set the cooking time to 60 minutes.
2. Hit Start/Stop button. While the unit is preheating, combine all meatloaf ingredients in a large mixing bowl.
3. When the unit beeps to indicate that it has been preheated, place the mixture on the Ninja Foodi Grill grate. Lock the hood and cook for 1 hour.
4. Prepare the sauce by mixing all the sauce ingredients together in a saucepan and bring to a boil.
5. Serve and enjoy!!!

Meatball Nirvana

Preparation Time: 20 minutes

Cook Time: 20 minutes

Total Time: 40 minutes

Serve: 4

Calories: 329 kcal

Ingredients:

- ¼ Cup of grated Parmesan cheese
- ½ Cup of seasoned bread crumbs
- 1 Lb. extra lean ground beef
- ½ Tsp. sea salt
- 1 Small onion, diced
- ½ Tsp. garlic salt
- 1 ½ Tsp. Italian seasoning
- ¾ Tsp. dried oregano
- ¾ Tsp. crushed red pepper flakes
- 1 Dash hot pepper sauce
- 1 ½ Tbsp. Worcestershire sauce
- ⅓ cup of skim milk

Cooking Instructions:

1. Preheat the unit by inserting the grill grate into the unit and lock the hood. Press Grill and set the temperature to Max. Set the cooking time to 20 minutes.
2. Hit Start/Stop button. While the unit is preheating, put the beef, salt, onion, garlic salt, Italian seasoning, and oregano.
3. Add red pepper flakes, hot pepper sauce, and Worcestershire sauce in a small mixing bowl. Give it a good stir.

4. Add the milk, Parmesan cheese, and bread crumbs. Stir thoroughly and then form into 1 ½" meatballs.
5. When the unit beeps to indicate that it has been preheated, arrange the meatballs in the Ninja Foodi Grill grate and lock the hood. Cook for 20 minutes.
6. Serve and enjoy!!!

Pulled Pork Hatch Chile Stew

Preparation Time: 25 minutes

Cook Time: 35 minutes

Total Time: 60 minutes

Serve: 6

Calories: 446 kcal

Ingredients:

- 2 Cups of Potatoes
- ½ Tsp. cumin
- 2 Tbsp. Canola Salad Oil ADM
- 1 Onions, raw
- 1 Cup of Carrots, raw
- 2 Hatch Chile peppers
- 3 Cloves of Garlic
- 1 Pinch of Salt
- 1 ½ Lb. cooked pork meat
- ¼ Cup of Wheat flour
- 4 Cups of Swanson Clear Chicken Broth CAM
- 1 (15 Oz.) Can Tomatoes, crushed

Cooking Instructions:

1. Preheat the unit by inserting the grill grate into the unit and lock the hood. Press Grill and set the temperature to Max. Set the cooking time to 35 minutes.
2. Hit Start/Stop button. When the unit beeps to indicate that it has been preheated, put onion, carrot, Chile peppers, garlic, salt and black pepper.
3. Stir in pork, flour and chicken broth. Put tomatoes, potatoes, and cumin. Lock the hood and cook for 35 minutes. Serve and enjoy!!!

Ninja Foodi Grill Fish & Seafood Recipes

Garlic Shrimp with Lemon

Preparation Time: 4 minutes

Cook Time: 15 minutes

Total Time: 19 minutes

Serve: 3

Calories: 228 kcal

Ingredients:

- Black pepper, to taste
- Lemon wedges
- 1 Lb. raw shrimp, peeled and deveined,
- Vegetable oil
- ¼ Tsp. garlic powder
- Salt, to taste

Cooking Instructions:

1. Preheat the unit by inserting the grill grate into the unit and lock the hood. Press Grill and set the temperature to Max. Set the cooking time to 15 minutes.
2. Hit Start/Stop button. While the unit is preheating, combine together the shrimp, oil, garlic powder, salt and pepper. Mix thoroughly.
3. When the unit beeps to indicate that it has been preheated, place the shrimp in the Ninja Foodi Grill grate. Lock the hood and cook for 15 minutes.
4. When the cooking cycle is over, remove the shrimp onto a serving platter and squeeze a little lemon into the shrimp.
5. Serve and enjoy!!!

Breaded Sea Scallops

Preparation Time: 10 minutes

Cook Time: 5 minutes

Total Time: 15 minutes

Serve: 4

Calories: 492 kcal

Ingredients:

- ½ Cup of Hi Ho Crackers-Crushed KBLR
- ½ Tsp. Spices, garlic powder
- ½ Tsp. Old Bay Seasoning TM
- 2 Tbsp. Butter, with salt
- 1 Lb. sea scallops

Cooking Instructions:

1. Preheat the unit by inserting the grill grate into the unit and lock the hood. Press Grill and set the temperature to Max. Set the cooking time to 5 minutes.
2. Hit Start/Stop button. While the unit is preheating, combine together the cracker crumbs, garlic powder, and seafood seasoning in a small mixing bowl.
3. Place melted butter in a second small mixing bowl. Bury each scallop in the melted butter and then roll in the breading mixture to be coated well.
4. When the unit beeps to indicate that it has been preheated, arrange scallops in the Ninja Foodi Grill grate. Lock the hood and cook for 5 minutes.
5. Serve and enjoy!!!

Crumbed Fish

Preparation Time: 10 minutes

Cook Time: 12 minutes

Total Time: 22 minutes

Serve: 4

Calories: 287 kcal

Ingredients:

- 1 Cup of Bread crumbs, dry, grated, plain
- ¼ Cup of Oil
- 4 Finfish, flatfish
- 1 Egg
- 1 Lemons, peeled

Cooking Instructions:

1. Preheat the unit by inserting the grill grate into the unit and lock the hood. Press Grill and set the temperature to Max. Set the cooking time to 12 minutes.
2. Hit Start/Stop button. While the unit is preheating, combine bread crumbs and oil together in a small mixing bowl. Stir thoroughly.
3. Bury fish fillets into the egg. Remove and dip fillets into the bread crumb mixture. When the unit beeps to indicate that it has been preheated, place the fillets in the Ninja Foodi Grill grate.
4. Lock the hood and cook for about 12 minutes. When it is completely cooked, flip fillets onto a serving plate and top with Lemon slices.
5. Serve and enjoy!!!

Alaska Salmon Bake with Pecan Crunch Coating

Preparation Time: 20 minutes

Cook Time: 10 minutes

Total Time: 30 minutes

Serve: 6

Calories: 428 kcal

Ingredients:

- 3 Tbsp. Dijon Mustard NB
- 3 Tbsp. Butter, with salt
- 5 Tsp. Honey
- ½ Cup of Bread crumbs, dried and grated
- ½ Cup of Nuts, pecans
- 3 Tsp. Parsley
- 6 (4 Oz.) Fillets sockeye salmon
- Salt
- 6 Wedge Lemons, peeled

Cooking Instructions:

1. Preheat the unit by inserting the grill grate into the unit and lock the hood. Press Grill and set the temperature to Max. Set the cooking time to 10 minutes.
2. Hit Start/Stop button. While the unit is preheating, combine the mustard, butter, and honey. In another bowl, merge together the bread crumbs, pecans, and parsley.
3. Apply each salmon fillet with salt and pepper. Place on the preheated Ninja Foodi Grill grate. Brush with mustard-honey mixture.
4. Cover the top of each fillet with bread crumb mixture. Close the hood and cook for 10 minutes. Top with lemon wedges. Serve and enjoy!!!

Baked Dijon Salmon

Preparation Time: 20 minutes

Cook Time: 15 minutes

Total Time: 35 minutes

Serve: 4

Calories: 288 kcal

Ingredients:

- ¼ Cup of butter, melted
- 3 Tbsp. Dijon mustard
- 1 ½ Tbsp. honey
- ¼ Cup of dry bread crumbs
- ¼ Cup of finely chopped pecans
- 4 Tsp. chopped fresh parsley
- 4 (4 Oz.) Fillets salmon
- Salt and pepper to taste
- 1 Lemon, for garnish

Cooking Instructions:

1. Preheat the unit by inserting the grill grate into the unit and lock the hood. Press Grill and set the temperature to Max. Set the cooking time to 15 minutes.
2. Hit Start/Stop button. While the unit is preheating, combine together butter, mustard, and honey in a small mixing bowl. Set aside.
3. Combine together the bread crumbs, pecans, and parsley in another small mixing bowl.
4. Rub each salmon fillet with honey mustard mixture, and sprinkle the top of the fillets with the bread crumb mixture.

5. When the unit beeps to indicate that it has been preheated, arrange the fillets in the Ninja Foodi Grill grate.
6. Close the hood and cook the fillets for 15 minutes. When it is done, season with salt and pepper and top with a wedge of lemon.
7. Serve and enjoy!!!

Barlow's Blackened Catfish

Preparation Time: 10 minutes

Cook Time: 40 minutes

Total Time: 50 minutes

Serve: 4

Calories: 296 kcal

Ingredients:

- 1 Cup of Salad Italian dressing
- 2 Tsp. Red pepper
- 2 Tsp. Lemon Pepper HS
- 2 Tsp. garlic powder
- 2 Tsp. Salt
- 2 Tsp. Ground black pepper
- 1 Lb. Finfish (catfish)
- 2 Tbsp. Butter

Cooking Instructions:

1. Preheat the unit by inserting the grill grate into the unit and lock the hood. Press Grill and set the temperature to Max. Set the cooking time to 40 minutes.
2. Press Start/Stop button. While the unit is preheating, combine together red pepper, lemon pepper, garlic powder, salt and pepper.
3. Rub butter on both sides of the catfish and then coat with the lemon mixture. When the unit is preheated, place the fillets on the Ninja Foodi Grill grate.
4. Coat with Italian-style salad dressing. Lock the hood and cook for 40 minutes. Flake with fork to check its doneness.
5. Serve and enjoy!!!

Perfect Fish

Preparation Time: 10 minutes

Cook Time: 10 minutes

Total Time: 20 minutes

Serve: 2

Calories: 331 kcal

Ingredients:

- 1 Lb. cod, cut into 4 strips
- Kosher salt
- Freshly ground black pepper
- ½ Cup of all-purpose flour
- 1 Large egg, beaten
- 2 Cup of panko bread crumbs
- 1 Tsp. Old Bay seasoning
- Lemon wedges
- Tartar sauce

Cooking Instructions:

1. Preheat the unit by inserting the grill grate into the unit and lock the hood. Press Grill and set the temperature to Max. Set the cooking time to 10 minutes.
2. Press Start/Stop button. While the unit is preheating, season fish with salt and pepper. Put flour, egg, and panko in three small mixing bowls.
3. Put Old Bay to panko and mix well. Coat fish with the flour, egg and panko mixture respectively.
4. When the unit beeps to indicate it is preheated, arrange the fish on the Ninja Foodi Grill grate. Lock the hood and cook for 10 minutes.
5. Top with lemon wedges and tartar sauce. Serve and enjoy!!!

Ninja Foodi Grill Soup Recipes

Broccoli Soup

Preparation Time: 10 minutes

Cook Time: 10 minutes

Total Time: 20 minutes

Serve: 4

Calories: 220 kcal

Ingredients:

- 1 Tbsp. olive oil
- 1 Medium white onion, peeled, chopped
- 3 Cups of vegetable broth
- 4 Cups of broccoli florets, cut in 1-inch pieces
- 1 Tsp. salt
- 1 Cup of shredded sharp cheddar cheese

Cooking Instructions:

1. Preheat the unit by inserting the grill grate into the unit and lock the hood. Press Grill and set the temperature to Max. Set the cooking time to 10 minutes.
2. Press Start/Stop button. When the unit is preheated, dump in onions, vegetable broth, broccoli, and salt.
3. Lock the hood and cook for about 10 minutes. When the cooking cycle is over, open the hood and stir in cheese. Cook for another 2 minutes.
4. Serve and enjoy!!!

Cauliflower Cheddar

Preparation Time: 10 minutes

Cook Time: 4 minutes

Total Time: 14 minutes

Serve: 4

Calories: 301 kcal

Ingredients:

- 3 Tbsp. unsalted butter
- 2 Cloves of garlic, peeled, chopped
- 1 Large onion, chopped
- ⅓ Cup of all-purpose flour
- 2 Tsp. salt
- 1 Tsp. ground black pepper
- 1 Large head cauliflower, cut into florets
- 5 Cups of vegetable broth
- 2 Cups of shredded cheddar cheese
- 2 Cups of milk

Cooking Instructions:

1. Preheat the unit by Inserting the grill grate into the unit and lock the hood. Press Grill and set the temperature to Max. Set the cooking time to 4 minutes.
2. Press Start/Stop button. When the unit is preheated, combine all the ingredients except cheese and milk into the unit. Lock the hood and cook for 20 minutes.
3. When the cooking cycle is over, open the hood and stir in cheese and milk. Stir thoroughly. Flip onto a serving plate.
4. Serve and enjoy!!!

Cauliflower Couscous

Preparation Time: 10 minutes

Cook Time: 7 minutes

Total Time: 17 minutes

Serve: 4

Calories: 411 kcal

Ingredients:

- 3 Cups of cauliflower florets
- 1 Clove of garlic, peeled
- 1 Tbsp. fresh rosemary
- ¼ Cup of extra virgin olive oil
- 2 Tsp. lemon juice
- ½ Tsp. salt
- ½ Tsp. ground black pepper
- ½ Cup of slivered almonds
- ¼ Cup of green onion, sliced

Cooking Instructions:

1. Preheat the unit by inserting the grill grate into the unit and lock the hood. Press Grill and set the temperature to Max. Set the cooking time to 7 minutes.
2. Press Start/Stop button. When the unit is preheated, put the cauliflower florets, garlic, and rosemary into a processor and chop the ingredients.
3. When the unit beeps to indicate that it has been preheated, arrange the cauliflower in the Ninja Foodi Grill grate.
4. Lock the hood and cook for about 7 minutes. When it is done, allow it to cool and then transfer cauliflower to a mixing bowl.
5. Add remaining ingredients and stir it properly. Serve and enjoy!!!

Classic Pea Soup

Preparation Time: 10 minutes

Cook Time: 10 minutes

Total Time: 20 minutes

Serve: 4

Calories: 119 kcal

Ingredients:

- 1 Cup of frozen peas, thawed
- 1 ½ Cups of low-sodium vegetable broth
- ¼ Medium onion
- 1 Stalk celery, cut in 1-inch pieces
- ½ Medium carrot, peeled, cut in 1-inch pieces
- ½ Tsp. salt
- ¼ Tsp. ground black pepper
- ¼ small bulb fennel, chopped

Cooking Instructions:

1. Preheat the unit by inserting the grill grate into the unit and lock the hood. Press Grill and set the temperature to Max. Set the cooking time to 10 minutes.
2. Press Start/Stop button. When the unit is preheated, put all ingredients in Tritan Nutri Ninja Cup according to how they are listed and blend for about 40 seconds.
3. When the unit is preheated, place soup in the Ninja Foodi Grill grate. Lock the hood and cook for 10 minutes.
4. Serve and enjoy!!!

Corn Soup with Chives

Preparation Time: 10 minutes

Cook Time: 10 minutes

Total Time: 20 minutes

Serve: 2

Calories: 430 kcal

Ingredients:

- 6 Ears corn, cooked, kernels cut off, cobs reserved
- Kosher salt to taste
- Pepper to taste
- Fresh chives, chopped

Cooking Instructions:

1. Preheat the unit by Inserting the grill grate into the unit and lock the hood. Press Grill and set the temperature to Max. Set the cooking time to 10 minutes.
2. Press Start/Stop button. When the unit is preheated, put the cooked corn into Tritan Nutri Ninja cups.
3. Put enough water into the cups and arrange them in the Ninja Foodi Grill grate. Lock the hood and cook for 10 minutes. Add salt and pepper. Top with chives.
4. Serve and enjoy!!!

Minestrone Soup

Preparation Time: 10 minutes

Cook Time: 2 minutes

Total Time: 12 minutes

Serve: 4

Calories: 367 kcal

Ingredients:

- 2 Cups of baby spinach
- 2 Tsp. lemon juice
- 2 Tbsp. extra virgin olive oil
- 1 Medium yellow onion, peeled and chopped
- 2 Stalks celery, chopped
- 4 Cloves of garlic, peeled and sliced
- Pinch of crushed red pepper
- 2 Tsp. kosher salt
- 1 Tsp. ground black pepper
- 2 Medium carrots, peeled, chopped
- 2 Yukon Gold potatoes, peeled, diced
- 1 Can of (14.5 Oz.) diced tomatoes
- ½ Tsp. dried oregano
- ½ Tsp. dried thyme
- 2 Bay leaves
- 4 Cups of vegetable broth
- 2 Cups of water
- 1 Can of (15 Oz.) red kidney beans, rinsed, drained
- Freshly grated Parmesan cheese

Cooking Instructions:

1. Preheat the unit by inserting the grill grate into the unit and lock the hood. Press Grill and set the temperature to Max. Set the cooking time to 2 minutes.
2. Press Start/Stop button. When the unit is preheated, add oil, onion, celery, garlic, crushed red pepper, salt, and pepper.
3. Put the remaining ingredients, except Parmesan. Lock the hood and cook for about 2 minutes. When cooking is complete, top with Parmesan cheese.
4. Serve and enjoy!!!

Smoky Black Bean Soup

Preparation Time: 10 minutes

Cook Time: 7 minutes

Total Time: 17 minutes

Serve: 4

Calories: 386 kcal

Ingredients:

- 1 Tbsp. canola oil
- 2 Cloves of garlic, peeled, chopped
- 1 Large onion, chopped
- 1 Red bell pepper, seeds removed, chopped
- 2 Cans of (15 Oz. each) black beans, rinsed, drained
- 1 Can (14 Oz.) diced tomatoes
- 2 Tbsp. smoked paprika
- 1 Tbsp. ground cumin
- 2 Tsp. salt
- 1 Tsp. ground black pepper
- 6 Cups of low-sodium vegetable broth

Cooking Instructions:

1. Preheat the unit by inserting the grill grate into the unit and lock the hood. Press Grill and set the temperature to Max. Set the cooking time to 7 minutes.
2. Press Start/Stop button. When the unit is preheated, place all the ingredients on the Ninja Foodi Grill grate and lock the hood. Cook for 7 minutes.
3. Immediately the cooking cycle is over, carefully puree the soup and turn the pureed soup to a serving plate.
4. Serve and enjoy!!!

Thai Pumpkin Soup

Preparation Time: 10 minutes

Cook Time: 5 minutes

Total Time: 15 minutes

Serve: 2

Calories: 215 kcal

Ingredients:

- 2 Tbsp. red curry paste
- ⅓ Cup of peanut butter
- 4 Cup of low sodium chicken broth
- 2 (15 Oz.) cans pumpkin puree
- 2 Cup of coconut milk

Cooking Instructions:

1. Preheat the unit by inserting the grill grate into the unit and lock the hood. Press Grill and set the temperature to Max. Set the cooking time to 5 minutes.
2. Press Start/Stop button. While the unit is preheating, place all the ingredients into a food processor and blend it to your desired consistency.
3. Transfer the mixture to the Ninja Foodi Grill grate. Lock the hood and cook for about 5 minutes. Ladle onto serving plates.
4. Serve and enjoy!!!

White Bean Turkey Chili

Preparation Time: 10 minutes

Cook Time: 25 minutes

Total Time: 35 minutes

Serve: 4

Calories: 476 kcal

Ingredients:

- 1 Jalapeño pepper, diced, seeds removed
- 1 Cup of shredded Monterey jack
- 1 Lb. uncooked ground turkey
- 1 Onion, peeled, diced
- 2 Tsp. chili powder
- 2 Tsp. ground cumin
- 2 Tsp. kosher salt
- 1 Tsp. ground black pepper
- 1 Can of (4 Oz.) green chilies
- 2 Cups of chicken stock
- 1 Bell pepper, diced, seeds removed
- 2 Cans of (15 Oz. each) white cannellini, undrained

Optional Toppings:

- Pepper jack cheese
- Avocado, diced
- Fresh cilantro, chopped
- Jalapeño peppers, sliced
- Sour cream
- Corn chips

Cooking Instructions:

1. Preheat the unit by inserting the grill grate into the unit and lock the hood. Press Grill and set the temperature to Max. Set the cooking time to 25 minutes.
2. Press Start/Stop button. While the unit is preheating, put the turkey, onion, spices, green chilies, and chicken stock to the Ninja Foodi Grill grate.
3. Break the turkey using wooden spoon. Add bell pepper, beans, and jalapeño pepper. Close the hood and cook for 25 minutes.
4. Open the hood and add shredded cheese. Give it a nice stir. Transfer the soup to a serving plate and garnish with toppings of your choice.
5. Serve and enjoy!!!

Ninja Foodi Grill Rice & Pasta Recipes

Garlic Herb Rice and Chicken

Preparation Time: 10 minutes

Cook Time: 20 minutes

Total Time: 30 minutes

Serve: 4

Calories: 221 kcal

Ingredients:

- 1 Box of garlic herb rice
- ½ Onion, chopped
- 1 Can of condensed cream of chicken
- 1 Can condensed cream of mushroom
- 1 Chopped roasted red pepper
- 2 Cans of mushrooms
- 1 Bag of steamed broccoli
- 3 Handful of Monterey Jack cheese
- Tub of Carly's sauce-less pulled chicken

Cooking Instructions:

1. Preheat the unit by inserting the grill grate into the unit and lock the hood. Press Grill and set the temperature to Max. Set the cooking time to 20 minutes.
2. Press Start/Stop button. When the unit is preheated, cook the garlic herb rice according to the direction on the box alongside with onion.
3. Put soup, red pepper, mushrooms, broccoli, and chicken into the Ninja Foodi Grill grate. Lock the hood, select Air Crisp and grill for 20 minutes.
4. Top with cheese. Serve and enjoy!!!

Garlic Chicken Breasts with Pasta

Preparation Time: 10 minutes

Cook Time: 30 minutes

Total Time: 40 minutes

Serve: 2

Calories: 379 kcal

Ingredients:

- 2 Chicken breasts cut into strips
- Garlic, onion spices, seasonings
- 1 Lb. of dry pasta, of your choice
- 4 Cups of water
- 1 (26 Oz.) jar of tomato sauce
- ½ Bag of spinach

Cooking Instructions:

1. Preheat the unit by inserting the grill grate into the unit and lock the hood. Press Grill and set the temperature to Max. Set the cooking time to 30 minutes.
2. Press Start/Stop button. While the unit is preheating, apply the seasoning on the chicken. When the unit beeps to indicate it is preheated, add pasta and water.
3. Put tomato sauce and half bag of spinach. Close the hood, select Air Crisp and then grill for 30 minutes.
4. Serve and enjoy!!!

Indian Rice Pilaf

Preparation Time: 10 minutes

Cook Time: 25 minutes

Total Time: 35 minutes

Serve: 2

Calories: 225 kcal

Ingredients:

- ¼ Cup of butter
- 2 Cloves of minced garlic
- 1 Cup of long grain rice
- 3 Cups beef broth
- Toasted almond slivers

Cooking Instructions:

1. Preheat the unit by inserting the grill grate into the unit and lock the hood. Press Grill and set the temperature to Max. Set the cooking time to 30 minutes.
2. Hit Start/Stop button. When the unit beeps to indicate that it is preheated, put butter, rice and garlic. Bring the rice to a broil.
3. Put beef broth. Give it a good mix. Lock the hood. Select Air Crisp and grill for 25 minutes. Top with toasted almond slivers and raisins.
4. Serve and enjoy!!!

Italian Sausage Pasta

Preparation Time: 10 minutes

Cook Time: 5 minutes

Total Time: 15 minutes

Serve: 4

Calories: 380 kcal

Ingredients:

- 2 Packages of Italian sausage, sliced
- 1 Red, yellow, and orange peppers, sliced
- 2 sweet onions, sliced
- 1 (8 Oz.) Can of sliced black olives
- A package of Bunapi mushrooms
- 2 (24 Oz.) Jars of garden variety Ragu spaghetti sauce
- Italian seasoning
- Oregeno
- Garlic
- A pinch of Salt
- Pepper to taste
- Mozzarella
- Parmesan cheese
- Chives

Cooking Instructions:

1. Preheat the unit by inserting the grill grate into the unit and lock the hood. Press Grill and set the temperature to Max. Set the cooking time to 5 minutes.
2. Hit Start/Stop button. When the unit beeps to indicate that it is preheated, put the spaghetti and place in a Ziploc bag with some cool water.

3. Bring to a broil. Remove and set aside. Put Italian sausage, onions, sweet peppers, and mushrooms into the Ninja Foodi Grill grate.
4. Add the black olives, Italian seasoning, garlic, oregano, salt, pepper and Ragu. Stir thoroughly and add the spaghetti.
5. Lock the hood and select Air Crisp. Grill for 5 minutes. When it is done, transfer onto a serving plate. Top with mozzarella, parmesan cheeses and chives.
6. Serve and enjoy!!!

Knorr Pasta Casserole

Preparation Time: 10 minutes

Cook Time: 50 minutes

Total Time: 60 minutes

Serve: 4

Calories: 331 kcal

Ingredients:

- ½ Package of Turkey bacon
- 2 Packages of Knorr pasta sides
- Chicken
- ½ Bag of frozen green beans
- Shredded cheddar cheese

Cooking Instructions:

1. Preheat the unit by inserting the grill grate into the unit and lock the hood. Press Grill and set the temperature to Max. Set the cooking time to 50 minutes.
2. Hit Start/Stop button. When the unit beeps to indicate that it is preheated, cook pasta according to package Instructions.
3. Dump in bacon, pasta, chicken and green beans. Lock the hood and select Air Crisp. Grill for an hour. Top with cheese.
4. Serve and enjoy!!!

Knorr Pasta Side Chicken Flavored Fettuccine

Preparation: 10 minutes

Cook Time: 25 minutes

Total Time: 35 minutes

Serve: 4

Calories: 260 kcal

Ingredients:

- 1 Packet of Knorr Pasta Side Chicken Flavored Fettuccine
- 2 Frozen chicken cutlets

Cooking Instructions:

1. Preheat the unit by inserting the grill grate into the unit and lock the hood. Press Grill and set the temperature to Max. Set the cooking time to 25 minutes.
2. Hit Start/Stop button. When the unit beeps to indicate that it is preheated, put the Knorr pasta side as directed on the package Instructions.
3. Give it a nice stir. Put the chicken into the Ninja Foodi Grill grate. Lock the hood and select Air Crisp. Grill for 25 minutes.
4. Serve and enjoy!!!

Ninja Foodi Grill Beans & Grain Recipes

Green Bean Casserole

Preparation: 10 minutes

Cook Time: 30 minutes

Total Time: 40 minutes

Serve: 4

Calories: 130 kcal

Ingredients:

- 1 (16 Oz.) Package of frozen cut green beans
- 1 (10.75 Oz.) Can cream of chicken soup cream of mushroom
- ⅓ Cup of milk
- ¼ Cup of grated Parmesan cheese
- ⅛ Tsp. salt
- ⅛ Tsp. ground black pepper
- ½ (6 Oz.) Can French-fried onions, divided

Cooking Instructions:

1. Preheat the unit by inserting the grill grate into the unit and lock the hood. Press Grill and set the temperature to Max. Set the cooking time to 30 minutes.
2. Hit Start/Stop button. When the unit beeps to indicate that it is preheated, dump in green beans, soup, milk, Parmesan cheese, salt, pepper, and onion.
3. Lock the hood and select Air Crisp. Grill for 30 minutes. Top casserole with remaining French-fried onions.
4. Serve and enjoy!!!

Ham, Green Beans and Potato Casserole

Preparation: 10 minutes

Cook Time: 35 minutes

Total Time: 45 minutes

Serve: 4

Calories: 388 kcal

Ingredients:

- 2 Lbs. fresh green beans, cut
- 4 Large baking potatoes, quartered
- 2 Lbs. ham, cut into cubes
- 3 Cups of water
- Seasonings of choice

Cooking Instructions:

1. Preheat the unit by inserting the grill grate into the unit and lock the hood. Press Grill and set the temperature to Max. Set the cooking time to 35 minutes.
2. Press Start/Stop button. When the unit beeps to indicate that it is preheated, put the green beans, potatoes and ham into the Ninja Foodi Grill grate.
3. Put water and seasoning. Lock the hood and select Air Crisp. Grill for 35 minutes. Transfer onto a serving plate.
4. Serve and enjoy!!!

Bean Dip

Preparation: 10 minutes

Cook Time: 1 minute

Total Time: 11 minutes

Serve: 4

Calories: 214 kcal

Ingredients:

- 1 Lb. ground beef
- 1 (15 Oz.) Can of re-fried beans
- 1 (4 Oz.) Can of diced green chilies
- ½ Lb. shredded jack cheese
- ½ Lb. shredded cheddar cheese
- 1 Onion finely chopped
- 1 Medium jar of salsa

Cooking Instructions:

1. Preheat the unit by inserting the grill grate into the unit and lock the hood. Press Grill and set the temperature to Max. Set the cooking time to 1 minute.
2. Press Start/Stop button. When the unit beeps to indicate that it is preheated, dump all the ingredients into the Ninja Foodi Grill grate and mix properly.
3. Close the hood and select Air Crisp. Grill for about 1 minute. When the cooking cycle is over, transfer to a serving plate and top with corn chips.
4. Serve and enjoy!!!

Black-Eyed Pea Cheese Dip

Preparation: 10 minutes

Cook Time: 1 minute

Total Time: 11 minutes

Serve: 2

Calories: 295 kcal

Ingredients:

- ½ Lb. ground sausage
- 1 Medium onion, chopped
- 4 Cloves of garlic, chopped
- 1 (15 Oz.) Can of black-eyed peas, drained
- 1 (10 Oz.) can RoTel
- 1 Tsp. chipotle chili powder
- 1 Lb. Velveeta, cut into 1-inch cubes
- Chips of choice

Cooking Instructions:

1. Preheat the unit by inserting the grill grate into the unit and lock the hood. Press Grill and set the temperature to Max. Set the cooking time to 1 minute.
2. Press Start/Stop button. When the unit beeps to indicate that it is preheated, dump all the ingredients into the Ninja Foodi Grill grate. Stir properly.
3. Lock the hood and select Air Crisp. Grill for 1 minute. When the cooking cycle is over, transfer onto a serving plate and top with chips of your choice.
4. Serve and enjoy!!!

Roasted Garbanzo Beans

Preparation: 10 minutes

Cook Time: 60 minutes

Total Time: 1 hour 10 minutes

Serve: 2

Calories: 439 kcal

Ingredients:

- 1 Can of Garbanzo beans, drained and towel dried
- 1 Tsp. olive oil
- Cajun seasoning

Cooking Instructions:

1. Preheat the unit by inserting the grill grate into the unit and lock the hood. Press Grill and set the temperature to Max. Set the cooking time to 60 minutes.
2. Press Start/Stop button. When the unit beeps to indicate that it is preheated, put the beans in a quart zip lock. Add the oil and seasoning. Give it a good stir.
3. Put the beans mixture in the Ninja Foodi Grill grate. Lock the hood and select Air Crisp. Grill for 1 hour.
4. Serve and enjoy!!!

Ninja Foodi Vegetable Recipes

Saffron, Courgette and Herb Couscous

Preparation: 10 minutes

Cook Time: 20 minutes

Total Time: 30 minutes

Serve: 6

Calories: 332 kcal

Ingredients:

- 350ml Homemade chicken stock
- 1 Tsp. salt
- ½ Tsp. freshly ground black pepper
- ¼ Tsp. ground cumin
- ½ Tsp. saffron threads
- 2 Tbsp. olive oil
- 30g Unsalted butter, melted
- 2 Courgettes, large dice
- 285g Couscous
- 20g Basil leaves, chopped
- 20g Parsley leaves, chopped

Cooking Instructions:

1. Preheat the unit by inserting the grill grate into the unit and lock the hood. Press Grill and set the temperature to Max. Set the cooking time to 20 minutes.
2. Hit Start/Stop button. When the unit beeps to indicate that it is preheated, add the salt, pepper, cumin, and saffron threads into the Ninja Foodi Grill grate.

3. Add the remaining ingredients except the parsley and Basil. Lock the hood and select Air Crisp. Grill for about 20 minutes.
4. When the cooking cycle is over, transfer onto a serving plate and top with Basil leaves and parsley.
5. Serve and enjoy!!!

Potato Soup

Preparation: 10 minutes

Cook Time: 20 minutes

Total Time: 30 minutes

Serve: 6

Calories: 350 kcal

Ingredients:

- ½ Large onion, diced
- 2 Stalks celery, diced
- 2 Medium carrots, diced
- 2 Cloves of garlic, minced
- 1 ½ Tsp. crushed rosemary, dried
- 5 Cups of diced red potatoes
- ¼ Cups of flour
- 3 ½ Cups of vegetable broth
- ½ Cup of heavy cream
- Salt
- Pepper

Cooking Instructions:

1. Preheat the unit by inserting the grill grate into the unit and lock the hood. Press Grill and set the temperature to Max. Set the cooking time to 20 minutes.
2. Hit Start/Stop button. When the unit beeps to indicate that it is preheated, add onions, celery, carrots, salt and pepper into the Ninja Foodi Grill grate. Stir.
3. Add garlic, rosemary, potatoes, and flour. Put the broth and give it a nice mix. Lock the hood and select Air Crisp. Grill for about 20 minutes.

4. Use an immersion blender to puree some of the veggies, and then add heavy cream. Adjust taste with salt and pepper.
5. Serve and enjoy!!!

Easy Kimchi Fried Rice

Preparation: 10 minutes

Cook Time: 20 minutes

Total Time: 30 minutes

Serve: 4

Calories: 297 kcal

Ingredients:

- 1 Tbsp. cooking oil
- 1 Medium onion, diced
- 1 Medium carrot, diced
- 2 Large garlic cloves, minced
- 1 (1") Cube ginger root, minced
- 1 Cup of kimchi, chopped
- ¼ Cup of kimchi juice
- 2 Tbsp. gochujang
- 1 Tbsp. soy Sauce
- 4 Cups of cooked long-grain white rice
- 2 Tsp. sesame oil
- 4 Fried eggs
- 2 Scallions (green parts only), chopped

Cooking Instructions:

1. Preheat the unit by inserting the grill grate into the unit and lock the hood. Press Grill and set the temperature to Max. Set the cooking time to 20 minutes.
2. Hit Start/Stop button. When the unit beeps to indicate that it is preheated, add onion, carrot, garlic and ginger, kimchi, kimchi juice, gochujang, and soy sauce.

3. Add rice and close the hood. Select Air Crisp and grill for about 20 minutes. Sprinkle with sesame oil. Share into 4 plates and top with fried egg and onion.
4. Serve and enjoy!!!

Vegetarian Pulled Pork

Preparation: 10 minutes

Cook Time: 10 minutes

Total Time: 20 minutes

Serve: 4

Calories: 425 kcal

Ingredients:

- 20 Oz. Young Green Jackfruit, drained
- ½ Tsp. Liquid Smoke
- 1 Cup of water vegetable broth
- 1 Cup of BBQ sauce
- 1 Tsp. Powder
- ½ Tsp. Onion Powder
- 1 Tsp. Paprika
- 1 ½ Tsp. of Salt
- Pepper to taste

Cooking Instructions:

1. Preheat the unit by inserting the grill grate into the unit and lock the hood. Press Grill and set the temperature to Max. Set the cooking time to 10 minutes.
2. Hit Start/Stop button. While the unit is preheating, pull the jackfruit apart, to resemble pulled pork using two forks.
3. When the unit beeps to indicate that it is preheated, place the jackfruit in the Foodi Grill grate and add salt, pepper, garlic, onion and paprika.
4. Put the vegetable broth and BBQ sauce. Stir it thoroughly. Lock the hood and select Air Crisp. Grill for about 10 minutes.
5. Serve and enjoy!!!

Toasted Israeli Couscous with Vegetables

Preparation: 30 minutes

Cook Time: 30 minutes

Total Time: 60 minutes

Serve: 4

Calories: 185 kcal

Ingredients:

- 225g Israeli couscous
- Salt
- 12 Spears asparagus, grilled and cut into ½ cm pieces
- 1 Courgette, halved, grilled and cut into 2 ½ cm pieces
- 1 Yellow squash, halved, grilled and cut into 2 ½ cm pieces
- 2 Large red peppers, grilled, peeled and diced into small pieces
- 40g Kalamata olives, pitted and chopped
- 2 Tbsp. chopped fresh basil leaves
- Freshly ground black pepper
- Lemon-balsamic vinaigrette

For the lemon-balsamic vinaigrette:

- 1 Small shallot, minced
- 3 Tbsp. fresh lemon juice
- 1 Tsp. lemon zest
- 3 Tbsp. aged balsamic vinegar
- 1 Tbsp. red wine vinegar
- Salt
- Freshly ground black pepper
- 190ml Extra-virgin olive oil

Cooking Instructions:

1. Preheat the unit by inserting the grill grate into the unit and lock the hood. Press Grill and set the temperature to Max. Set the cooking time to 30 minutes.
2. Hit Start/Stop button. When the unit beeps to indicate it is preheated, dump all the ingredients into the Ninja Foodi Grill grate except the Basil, olive and vinaigrette.
3. Add ½ liter of water. Lock the hood and select Air Crisp. Grill for 30 minutes. Open the hood and sprinkle with salt and pepper.
4. Serve and enjoy!!!

Ninja Foodi Grill Appetizer Recipes

Boiled Cajun Peanuts

Preparation: 10 minutes

Cook Time: 60 minutes

Total Time: 1 hour 10 minutes

Serve: 3

Calories: 185 kcal

Ingredients:

- 1 Lb. raw peanuts, in shells
- 1 (3 Oz.) Package of dry crab boil
- ½ Cup of chopped jalapeno peppers
- 1 Tbsp. garlic powder
- ½ Cup of salt
- 2 Tbsp. Cajun seasoning
- ½ Cup of red pepper flakes

Cooking Instructions:

1. Preheat the unit by inserting the grill grate into the unit and lock the hood. Press Grill and set the temperature to Max. Set the cooking time to 60 minutes.
2. Press Start/Stop button. When the unit beeps to indicate that it is preheated, put peanuts, crab boil, jalapenos, garlic powder, salt, Cajun seasoning, and red pepper flakes into the Ninja Foodi Grill grate.
3. Pour water to cover the peanuts and give it a good stir. Lock the hood and select Air Crisp. Grill for about 60 minutes.
4. Serve and enjoy!!!

Bourbon Infused Meatballs

Preparation: 10 minutes

Cook Time: 10 minutes

Total Time: 20 minutes

Serve: 4

Calories: 270 kcal

Ingredients:

- 32 Oz. bag frozen meatballs
- 2 Cups of barbecue sauce
- 1 Cups of bourbon
- 1 Cups of yellow mustard
- 1 Cups of honey
- 1 Tsp. garlic powder
- 1 Tsp. dried onion flakes
- 3 Tbsp. lemon juice
- ¼ Tsp. Worcestershire sauce

Cooking Instructions:

1. Preheat the unit by inserting the grill grate into the unit and lock the hood. Press Grill and set the temperature to Max. Set the cooking time to 10 minutes.
2. Press Start/Stop button. While the unit is preheating, merge together all the ingredients in a medium mixing bowl. Give it a good mix.
3. Put frozen meatballs in the Ninja Foodi Grill grate. Pour the sauce over them. Lock the hood and select Air Crisp. Grill for 10 minutes.
4. Serve and enjoy!!!

Buffalo Chicken Dip

Preparation: 10 minutes

Cook Time: 10 minutes

Total Time: 20 minutes

Serve: 4

Calories: 270 kcal

Ingredients:

- 2 Lbs. chicken cut in cubes
- 4 Cups of shredded cheddar cheese
- 2 (8 Oz.) Packages of light cream cheese
- 1 12 Oz. small jar of blue cheese dressing
- 2 Cups of Franks hot sauce

Cooking Instructions:

1. Preheat the unit by inserting the grill grate into the unit and lock the hood. Press Grill and set the temperature to Max. Set the cooking time to 10 minutes.
2. Press Start/Stop button. When the unit beeps to indicate that it is preheated, put all the ingredients into the Ninja Foodi Grill grate.
3. Lock the hood and select Air Crisp. Grill for about 10 minutes. When the cooking cycle is over, transfer onto a serving plate.
4. Serve and enjoy!!!

Buffalo Wings

Preparation: 10 minutes

Cook Time: 10 minutes

Total Time: 20 minutes

Serve: 4

Calories: 311 kcal

Ingredients:

- 4 Lbs. of wings, frozen
- 12 Oz. of Buffalo sauce

Cooking Instructions:

1. Preheat the unit by inserting the grill grate into the unit and lock the hood. Press Grill and set the temperature to Max. Set the cooking time to 10 minutes.
2. Press Start/Stop button. When the unit beeps to indicate that it is preheated, add the two ingredients into the Ninja Foodi Grill grate.
3. Lock the hood and select Air Crisp. Grill for about 10 minutes. When the cooking cycle is over, transfer onto a serving plate.
4. Serve and enjoy!!!

Easy BBQ Meatball

Preparation: 10 minutes

Cook Time: 15 minutes

Total Time: 25 minutes

Serve: 2

Calories: 224 kcal

Ingredients:

- 1 - 14 Oz. package frozen meatballs
- 1- 12 Oz. jar of grape jelly
- 1- 8 Oz. Bottle of Sweet Baby Rays BBQ sauce

Cooking Instructions:

1. Preheat the unit by inserting the grill grate into the unit and lock the hood. Press Grill and set the temperature to Max. Set the cooking time to 15 minutes.
2. Press Start/Stop button. When the unit beeps to indicate that it is preheated, put the grape jelly and barbeque sauce into the Ninja Foodi Grill grate. Stir properly.
3. Put the meatballs. Close the hood and select Air Crisp. Grill for about 15 minutes. When the cooking cycle is over, transfer onto a serving plate.
4. Serve and enjoy!!!

Honey-Glazed Shoyu Chicken Wings

Preparation: 10 minutes

Cook Time: 45 minutes

Total Time: 55 minutes

Serve: 3

Calories: 366 kcal

Ingredients:

- 6 Tbsp. soy sauce
- 1 Tbsp. honey
- 1 Tbsp. sesame oil
- 1 Tbsp. red pepper flakes
- ½ Tsp. garlic powder
- ½ Tsp. onion powder

Cooking Instructions:

1. Preheat the unit by inserting the grill grate into the unit and lock the hood. Press Grill and set the temperature to Max. Set the cooking time to 15 minutes.
2. Press Start/Stop button. While the unit is preheating, merge together all the ingredients in a small mixing bowl. Remain some for brushing on chicken.
3. Put the chicken in a Ziploc bag and pour marinade over chicken. Allow it to marinate for one hour.
4. Put a cup of water into the unit and place the chicken in the Ninja Foodi Grill grate. Close the hood and select Air Crisp. Grill for 45 minutes.
5. After 20 minutes of cooking cycle, remove the chicken and brush with the reserved marinade.
6. Replace the chicken in the Ninja Foodi Grill grate and continue cooking. Serve and enjoy!!!

Honey Lemon Chicken Wings

Preparation: 10 minutes

Cook Time: 50 minutes

Total Time: 60 minutes

Serve: 4

Calories: 186 kcal

Ingredients:

- 2 Dozen of wings
- 2 Chopped green onions

For the Sauce:

- ½ cup of lemon juice
- ½ Cup of honey
- ½ Stick of butter, melted
- Chili pepper flakes

Cooking Instructions:

1. Preheat the unit by inserting the grill grate into the unit and lock the hood. Press Grill and set the temperature to Max. Set the cooking time to 50 minutes.
2. Hit Start/Stop button. While the unit is preheating, merge together all the sauce ingredients in a small mixing bowl and set aside.
3. Season the wings with your choice of seasonings and place the chicken in the Ninja Foodi Grill grate.
4. Lock the hood and select Air Crisp. Grill for 50 minutes. After 20 minutes of cooking cycle, add sauce and still.
5. Continue cooking until it is properly cooked. Top with onion.
6. Serve and enjoy!!!

Jalapeno Poppers

Preparation: 10 minutes

Cook Time: 20 minutes

Total Time: 30 minutes

Serve: 2

Calories: 330 kcal

Ingredients:

- Crescent rolls
- 2 Minced jalapenos
- 1 8 Oz. cream cheese
- Garlic powder
- Bacon bits

Cooking Instructions:

1. Preheat the unit by inserting the grill grate into the unit and lock the hood. Press Grill and set the temperature to Max. Set the cooking time to 50 minutes.
2. Hit Start/Stop button. While the unit is preheating, combine all the ingredients together and unroll ½ tube of crescent. Keep 2 of the crescents together.
3. Pinch together the seams. Spread mixture over and roll up jellyroll style. Slice to look like the tortilla roll ups.
4. Place them in the Ninja Foodi Grill grate. Lock the hood and select Air Crisp. Grill for about 20 minutes.
5. Serve and enjoy!!!

Meatballs with Spinach, Mushrooms Sauce

Preparation: 10 minutes

Cook Time: 30 minutes

Total Time: 40 minutes

Serve: 4

Calories: 198 kcal

Ingredients:

- 10 Oz. chopped spinach
- 16 Oz. meatballs
- 24 Oz. jar sauce
- 2 Tbsp. minced garlic
- 8 Oz. sliced mushrooms
- ½ Cup of diced onion
- 1 Tbsp. olive oil
- Parmesan cheese

Cooking Instructions:

1. Preheat the unit by inserting the grill grate into the unit and lock the hood. Press Grill and set the temperature to Max. Set the cooking time to 30 minutes.
2. Hit Start/Stop button. When the unit beeps to indicate that it is preheated, put oil, meatballs, onions and mushrooms.
3. Put the sauce and spinach. Close the hood and select Air Crisp. Grill for about 30 minutes. Top with Parmesan cheese.
4. Serve and enjoy!!!

Mozzarella Stuffed Meatballs

Preparation: 10 minutes

Cook Time: 25 minutes

Total Time: 35 minutes

Serve: 4

Calories: 298 kcal

Ingredients:

- Mozzarella cheese, cut into ¾ inch cubes
- Marina
- 1 Lb. ground beef
- 1 Lb. hot Italian sausage
- ½ Tsp. garlic powder
- 2 Tsp. salt
- 1 Tsp. black pepper
- 1 Cup of bread crumbs
- ¼ Cup of parmesan cheese
- 2 Eggs
- ½ Cup of whole milk
- ½ Cup of chopped parsley

Cooking Instructions:

1. Preheat the unit by inserting the grill grate into the unit and lock the hood. Press Grill and set the temperature to Max. Set the cooking time to 25 minutes.
2. Hit Start/Stop button. While the unit is preheating, merge together all the ingredients in a large mixing bowl except the Mozzarella and marina.
3. Roll the beef mixture into golf ball sized balls. Squish a mozzarella cube into the center and close the edges.

4. Place the meatballs in the Ninja Foodi Grill grate. Close the hood and select Air Crisp. Grill for 25 minutes.
5. Serve and enjoy!!!

Party Meatballs

Preparation: 10 minutes

Cook Time: 40 minutes

Total Time: 50 minutes

Serve: 2

Calories: 448 kcal

Ingredients:

- 1 (28 Oz.) Bag of frozen meatballs meat balls
- 1 (18 Oz.) Jar of grape jelly
- 1 (12 Oz.) Jar of chili sauce
- 1 (18 Oz.) Bottle of BBQ sauce
- 1 Large vidalia onion, chopped

Cooking Instructions:

1. Preheat the unit by inserting the grill grate into the unit and lock the hood. Press Grill and set the temperature to Max. Set the cooking time to 40 minutes.
2. Hit Start/Stop button. While the unit is preheating, merge together the Onion, grape jelly, BBQ sauce, and chili sauce in small mixing bowl. Mix properly.
3. Put the sauce into the Ninja Foodi Grill grate alongside with the onion mixture. Put meatballs and give it a good stir.
4. Lock the hood and select Air Crisp. Grill for about 40 minutes. When the cooking cycle is over, transfer onto a serving plate.
5. Serve and enjoy!!!

Pillsbury Crescent Rolls with Pepperoni and String Cheese

Preparation: 10 minutes

Cook Time: 20 minutes

Total Time: 30 minutes

Serve: 1

Calories: 220 kcal

Ingredients:

- Pepperoni
- String cheese
- Crescent rolls

Cooking Instructions:

1. Preheat the unit by inserting the grill grate into the unit and lock the hood. Press Grill and set the temperature to Max. Set the cooking time to 20 minutes.
2. Hit Start/Stop button. While the unit is preheating, Place ½ stick of cheese and pepperoni on crescent dough and roll up.
3. Put the rolled crescents in the Ninja Foodi Grill grate. Lock the hood and select Air Crisp. Grill for 20 minutes.
4. Serve and enjoy!!!

Sausage and Cheese

Preparation: 10 minutes

Cook Time: 10 minutes

Total Time: 20 minutes

Serve: 1

Calories: 255 kcal

Ingredients:

- 1 Lb. breakfast sausage
- 1 Lb. Velveeta, cubed
- Party rye
- Pumpernickel

Cooking Instructions:

1. Preheat the unit by inserting the grill grate into the unit and lock the hood. Press Grill and set the temperature to Max. Set the cooking time to 10 minutes.
2. Hit Start/Stop button. When the unit beeps to indicate it is preheated, add the sausage and then Velveeta cubes to the sausage. Stir thoroughly.
3. Put mounds on Party Rye or Pumpernickel. Lock the hood and select Air Crisp. Grill for 10 minutes.
4. Serve and enjoy!!!

Spinach Artichoke Dip

Preparation: 10 minutes

Cook Time: 30 minutes

Total Time: 40 minutes

Serve: 4

Calories: 445 kcal

Ingredients:

- 1 Cup of Parmesan cheese
- 1 Tsp. minced garlic
- 10 Oz. frozen package chopped spinach-thawed and squeezed dry
- 14 Oz. jar artichoke hearts chopped
- 16 Oz. jar Ragu 4 cheese sauce
- 4 Oz. room temperature cream cheese
- ½ Cup of mozzarella cheese-grated

Cooking Instructions:

1. Preheat the unit by inserting the grill grate into the unit and lock the hood. Press Grill and set the temperature to Max. Set the cooking time to 30 minutes.
2. Hit Start/Stop button. When the unit beeps to indicate it is preheated, add all the ingredients into the Ninja Foodi Grill grate.
3. Lock the hood and select Air Crisp. Grill for 30 minutes. When the cooking cycle is over, transfer the dip onto a serving plate.
4. Serve and enjoy!!!

Steak and Beef Nachos

Preparation: 10 minutes

Cook Time: 5 minutes

Total Time: 15 minutes

Serve: 4

Calories: 380 kcal

Ingredients:

- 1 Lb. of ground beef
- 1 Taco seasoning pack
- ⅔ Cup of beef broth
- John Soules frozen beef steak strips
- 1 15 Oz. jar of cheese dip
- Tortilla chips

Cooking Instructions:

1. Preheat the unit by inserting the grill grate into the unit and lock the hood. Press Grill and set the temperature to Max. Set the cooking time to 5 minutes.
2. Hit Start/Stop button. When the unit beeps to indicate it is preheated, add the ground beef, taco seasoning pack with beef broth.
3. Put your desired amount of frozen beef steak strips. Add the cheese dip. Close the hood and select Air Crisp.
4. Grill for 5 minutes. When the cooking cycle is over, transfer the dip onto a serving plate and top with your desired toppings.
5. Serve and enjoy!!!

Ninja Foodi Grill Dessert Recipes

Baked Drunken Apples

Preparation: 10 minutes

Cook Time: 30 minutes

Total Time: 40 minutes

Serve: 4

Calories: 232 kcal

Ingredients:

- 7 Medium sized apples, cored halfway
- 1 Cup of ginger ale soda
- 1 Cup of brown sugar
- ⅓ Cup of raisins
- ⅓ Cup of walnuts, chopped
- ½ Cup of whiskey
- Cinnamon

Cooking Instructions:

1. Preheat the unit by inserting the grill grate into the unit and lock the hood. Press Grill and set the temperature to Max. Set the cooking time to 30 minutes.
2. Hit Start/Stop button. When the unit beeps to indicate it is preheated, place the apples into the Ninja Foodi Grill grate.
3. Merge together the brown sugar, raisins and walnuts in a small mixing bowl. Mix well and stuff into the apples. Pour whiskey and ginger ale together in a bowl.
4. Add remaining sugar, raisin and walnut mixture. Give it a nice mix. Pour on top of the apples and top with cinnamon.

5. Lock the hood and select Air Crisp. Cook for about 30 minutes. When cooking cycle is up, transfer onto a serving plate.
6. Serve and enjoy!!!

Pumpkin Cake

Preparation: 10 minutes

Cook Time: 50 minutes

Total Time: 60 minutes

Serve: 2

Calories: 190 kcal

Ingredients:

- 1 Yellow cake mix
- 1 Tbsp. pumpkin pie spice
- 1 Can pumpkin
- 1 Cup of dried cranberries
- ½ Bag of dark chocolate chips

Cooking Instructions:

1. Preheat the unit by inserting the grill grate into the unit and lock the hood. Press Grill and set the temperature to Max. Set the cooking time to 50 minutes.
2. Hit Start/Stop button. While the unit is preheating, merge all the ingredients together in a small mixing bowl. Stir thoroughly.
3. When the unit beeps to indicate that it is preheated, pour the mixture into the Ninja Foodi Grill grate. Lock the hood and select Air Crisp. Grill for 50 minutes.
4. Serve and enjoy!!!

Apple Cobbler

Preparation: 10 minutes

Cook Time: 25 minutes

Total Time: 35 minutes

Serve: 2

Calories: 339 kcal

Ingredients:

- 2 Cups of apples, diced
- 2 Cups of milk
- 2 Cups of sugar
- 2 Cups of flour
- 2 Tbsp. of butter, melted
- Cinnamon
- Vanilla

Cooking Instructions:

1. Preheat the unit by inserting the grill grate into the unit and lock the hood. Press Grill and set the temperature to Max. Set the cooking time to 25 minutes.
2. Hit Start/Stop button. While the unit is preheating, merge all the ingredients in a small mixing bowl except the apples.
3. Put the mixture into the Ninja Foodi Grill grate. Dump in apples into the mixture. Close the hood and select Air Crisp. Grill for about 25 minutes.
4. Serve and enjoy!!!

Banana Cupcakes

Preparation: 10 minutes

Cook Time: 20 minutes

Total Time: 30 minutes

Serve: 2

Calories: 305 kcal

Ingredients:

- 3 Large bananas
- 1 Box of cake mix

Cooking Instructions:

1. Preheat the unit by inserting the grill grate into the unit and lock the hood. Press Grill and set the temperature to Max. Set the cooking time to 20 minutes.
2. Press Start/Stop button. While the unit is preheating, marsh the bananas and add the cake mix. Give it a thorough stir.
3. Pour the mixture into the cup cake pan and place it in the Ninja Foodi Grill grate. Close the hood and select Air Crisp. Cook for 20 minutes.
4. Serve and enjoy!!!

Black Bean Brownies

Preparation: 10 minutes

Cook Time: 20 minutes

Total Time: 30 minutes

Serve: 2

Calories: 305 kcal

Ingredients:

- 15 Oz. can undrained black beans
- 1 Box brownie mix

Cooking Instructions:

1. Preheat the unit by inserting the grill grate into the unit and lock the hood. Press Grill and set the temperature to Max. Set the cooking time to 20 minutes.
2. Press Start/Stop button. When the unit beeps to indicate that it is preheated, put the 2 ingredients into the Ninja Foodi Grill grate.
3. Close the hood and select Air Crisp. Grill for 20 minutes. When the cooking cycle is over, transfer onto a serving plate.
4. Serve and enjoy!!!

Blueberry Lemon Thyme Crisp

Preparation: 10 minutes

Cook Time: 40 minutes

Total Time: 50 minutes

Serve: 2

Calories: 328 kcal

Ingredients:

- 1 Cup of fresh blueberries
- 5 Tsp. Sugar
- 1 Lemon
- 5 Tsp. Thyme
- Corn starch
- Pre-packaged Blueberry granola

Cooking Instructions:

1. Preheat the unit by inserting the grill grate into the unit and lock the hood. Press Grill and set the temperature to Max. Set the cooking time to 40 minutes.
2. Press Start/Stop button. While the unit is preheating, merge together the blueberries, sugar and thyme, corn starch in a small mixing bowl. Mix thoroughly.
3. Brush the grill grate with cooking spray and pour the mixture into it. ts. Place granola into a bowl and add 5 pieces of butter. Mix it with your hands.
4. Pour the mixture on top of the blueberries. Close the hood and select Air Crisp. Grill for 40 minutes.
5. Serve and enjoy!!!

Cherry Dump Cake

Preparation: 15 minutes

Cook Time: 40 minutes

Total Time: 55 minutes

Serve: 2

Calories: 197 kcal

Ingredients:

- 1 Box yellow cake mix
- 2 (21 Oz.) Cans of cherry pie filling
- 1 Stick melted butter

Cooking Instructions:

1. Preheat the unit by inserting the grill grate into the unit and lock the hood. Press Grill and set the temperature to Max. Set the cooking time to 40 minutes.
2. Press Start/Stop button. When the unit beeps to indicate that it is preheated, pour the cans of cherries into the Ninja Foodi Grill grate.
3. Merge together the cake mix and melted butter in a small mixing bowl and then pour batter over cherries.
4. Close the hood and select Air Crisp. Grill for about 40 minutes. When the cooking cycle is over, transfer onto a serving plate and top with ice cream.
5. Serve and enjoy!!!

Chocolate Cobbler

Preparation: 15 minutes

Cook Time: 30 minutes

Total Time: 45 minutes

Serve: 6

Calories: 274 kcal

Ingredients:

- ¾ Cup of butter, melted
- ½ Cup of milk
- 3 Cups of sugar, divided
- 1 ½ Cups of self-rising flour
- 1 Cup of baking cocoa, divided
- 2 Tsp. vanilla extract
- 2½ Cups of boiling water

Cooking Instruction:

1. Preheat the unit by inserting the grill grate into the unit and lock the hood. Press Grill and set the temperature to Max. Set the cooking time to 30 minutes.
2. Press Start/Stop button. While the unit is preheating, mix together 1½ cups of the sugar, flour, milk, ½ cup of cocoa and vanilla in a large mixing bowl and pour over butter.
3. Merge together remaining sugar and cocoa in a small mixing bowl and sprinkle over the batter. Pour boiling water over the top. Do not mix.
4. Place the mixture in the Ninja Foodi Grill grate. Lock the hood and select Air Crisp. Grill for 30 minutes.
5. Serve and enjoy!!!

Chocolate Lava Cake

Preparation: 15 minutes

Cook Time: 15 minutes

Total Time: 30 minutes

Serve: 4

Calories: 338 kcal

Ingredients:

Cake:

- 1 Box Betty Crocker Super Moist triple chocolate fudge cake mix
- 1¼ Cups of milk
- ½ Cup of vegetable oil

Topping:

- 1 Box of instant chocolate pudding and pie filling mix
- 2 Cups of milk
- 1 Bag of (12 Oz.) milk chocolate chips (2 cups)

Cooking Instructions:

1. Preheat the unit by inserting the grill grate into the unit and lock the hood. Press Grill and set the temperature to Max. Set the cooking time to 15 minutes.
2. Press Start/Stop button. While the unit is preheating, mix together, beat cake ingredients into a large mixing bowl.
3. Brush the Ninja Foodi Grill grate with cooking oil and pour the mixture into the grill grate.
4. Beat pudding mix and 2 cups of milk into a medium mixing bowl. Pour the mixture over the cake batter. Sprinkle chocolate chips over top. Do not mix.

5. Close the hood and select Air Crisp. Grill for 15 minutes. When the cooking cycle is over, remove the cake onto a serving plate.
6. Serve and enjoy!!!

www.ingramcontent.com/pod-product-compliance
Lightning Source LLC
Chambersburg PA
CBHW081751100526
44592CB00015B/2388